Schooling During a Pandemic

THE EXPERIENCE AND OUTCOMES OF SCHOOLCHILDREN DURING THE FIRST ROUND OF COVID-19 LOCKDOWNS

William Thorn and Stéphan Vincent-Lancrin

This work is published under the responsibility of the Secretary-General of the OECD. The opinions expressed and arguments employed herein do not necessarily reflect the official views of OECD member countries.

This document, as well as any data and map included herein, are without prejudice to the status of or sovereignty over any territory, to the delimitation of international frontiers and boundaries and to the name of any territory, city or area.

The statistical data for Israel are supplied by and under the responsibility of the relevant Israeli authorities. The use of such data by the OECD is without prejudice to the status of the Golan Heights, East Jerusalem and Israeli settlements in the West Bank under the terms of international law.

Note by Turkey
The information in this document with reference to "Cyprus" relates to the southern part of the Island. There is no single authority representing both Turkish and Greek Cypriot people on the Island. Turkey recognises the Turkish Republic of Northern Cyprus (TRNC). Until a lasting and equitable solution is found within the context of the United Nations, Turkey shall preserve its position concerning the "Cyprus issue".

Note by all the European Union Member States of the OECD and the European Union
The Republic of Cyprus is recognised by all members of the United Nations with the exception of Turkey. The information in this document relates to the area under the effective control of the Government of the Republic of Cyprus.

Please cite this publication as:
Thorn, W. and S. Vincent-Lancrin (2021), *Schooling During a Pandemic: The Experience and Outcomes of Schoolchildren During the First Round of COVID-19 Lockdowns*, OECD Publishing, Paris, *https://doi.org/10.1787/1c78681e-en*.

ISBN 978-92-64-50450-9 (print)
ISBN 978-92-64-57901-9 (pdf)

Photo credits: Cover © Silvia Camporesi, "Parco", 2020, courtesy of the Italian Ministry of Culture.

Corrigenda to publications may be found on line at: *www.oecd.org/about/publishing/corrigenda.htm*.
© OECD 2021

The use of this work, whether digital or print, is governed by the Terms and Conditions to be found at *http://www.oecd.org/termsandconditions*.

Foreword

After 18 months of disruption caused by the COVID-19 pandemic at students, teachers and parents, in most OECD countries, can look forward to a return to something close to "normal" in schools. However, even in the absence of further disruption, as they move forward, education systems will need to deal with the effects of past disruption on students' learning and well-being. What evidence do we have regarding these effects?

Since the beginning of the pandemic, the OECD has actively monitored the response of education systems and the measures implemented by governments to support learning during the crisis, both at the school and higher education levels. It has also documented, in real time, a host of country initiatives across the globe showing how a variety of actors, both governmental and non-governmental, worked together to support students and families in their learning while schools were closed.

This report looks at the consequences of the pandemic on schooling from a different perspective by focusing on the experience of children (and their families) during the first wave of school closures in the first half of 2020. How did children and their families deal with the sudden lockdowns and school closures? How did they manage the challenges of home-based schooling in the context of stay at home orders, strict restrictions on social contacts and mobility, and dramatic changes to the working arrangements of parents? The evidence suggests that while this period had its negative aspects, it also had its positive side. Overall, the picture presented in this report is relatively optimistic, offering a testimony to the adaptability and resilience of schoolchildren, their parents/guardians and their teachers.

Distance/remote education arrangements were put in place in emergency conditions. While by no means a perfect substitute for normal classes, they, nevertheless, ensured that most, though not all, children continued to have a connection with teachers and their schools. For the most part, teachers, students and parents adapted to the new arrangements. Most teachers continued to teach and most students continued to learn. Most parents were able to assist their children with their education if needed.

The experience of this period varied across social groups. While the majority of schoolchildren and their families negotiated this period without serious adverse effects on learning or well-being, this was not true for all. There is some evidence that the negative effects were greatest for children from less advantaged backgrounds.

For the moment, any assessment of the educational effects of the pandemic and the measures taken to control is, inevitably, provisional. The data available are limited in some important areas. For example, many countries suspended national testing programmes in 2020. Consequently, comparisons of achievement prior to and during or immediately after the pandemic-related disruptions exist in only a small number of countries and jurisdictions. In addition, disruptions to schooling of various types continued well into 2021 in many OECD countries. Equally importantly, most school systems took action designed to compensate for instruction that was missed during the school closures. Only by following the cohorts affected by the COVID-19 pandemic over a relatively long period can any lasting effects be identified.

The results of national testing programmes reinstated after their suspension in 2020 will provide vital information, as will international assessments such as the OECD Programme for International Student

Assessment (PISA), which will collect data in 2022. In the meantime, this report provides initial food for thought to look to the future while learning from positives and negatives of how students, families and schools adapted to this unprecedented situation.

Andreas Schleicher

Director for Education and Skills

Acknowledgements

This report was written by William Thorn and Stéphan Vincent-Lancrin, both Senior Analysts at the OECD Directorate for Education and Skills.

Vivien Liu provided excellent research assistance and reviewed most existing studies on the first wave of lockdowns while doing an internship at the OECD. Gwénaël Jacotin and Vanessa Denis, Statisticians at the OECD, helped with the analysis and presentation of data. Sabrina Leonarduzzi prepared the report for publication. Alison Burke managed the publication process.

Andreas Schleicher, Director for Education and Skills, and Dirk Van Damme, former Head of CERI, provided feedback on the report.

The report is an output of the OECD Centre for Educational Research and Innovation's (CERI) "COVID-19 R&D Fund", which was set up to analyse in a responsive way the educational impact of the COVID-19 pandemic. The report benefited from the comments of members of the CERI Governing Board on a first draft of the report: they are thankfully acknowledged. In particular, colleagues from France provided detailed comments. OECD member countries were also asked to check and provide any missing statistical study concerning their country.

The photo on the cover of this publication is a work ("Parco, 2020") by the Italian artist, Silvia Camporesi. It is one of a series of photos taken by the artist in April 2020 during the period of lockdown in Italy. Camporesi was one of a group of Italian photographers of different generations commissioned to contribute to a project intended to create a visual archive of Italy during the health crisis. The project was supported by the Italian Ministry of Culture. The work of the photographers concerned has been shown in an exhibition entitled "Italia in attesa" ("Italy on hold") at the Palazzo Barberini in Rome.

Table of contents

Foreword — 3

Acknowledgements — 5

Executive summary — 9

1 Introduction — 12
Schooling during a pandemic: An initial overview — 13
Data sources — 13
References — 14
Notes — 15

2 Aspects of schooling during lockdowns — 16
Two months of home-based schooling — 17
The delivery of instruction and instructional materials — 18
Learning time during school closures — 23
Parental and family involvement — 27
The challenges of home-based schooling for students — 32
Summary — 33
References — 34
Notes — 38

3 Lockdowns and the home environment — 40
Introduction — 41
Employment and working arrangements of parents — 41
Financial stress — 46
The health situation in families — 48
Family relationships — 52
Summary — 54
References — 55
Notes — 60

4 School children's psychological well-being and academic progress — 62
Introduction — 63
The psychological well-being of children — 63
Home learning: Parents', teachers and students' perceptions — 66
Evidence from standardised achievement tests — 73
Summary — 84

| References | 85 |
| Notes | 88 |

5 Summary and conclusions — 90
  Introduction — 91
  What do we know? — 91
  Looking ahead — 95
  References — 98
  Notes — 98

Annex A. Main survey data sources — 100

Annex B. Lockdown measures in selected countries: February-June 2020 — 105
  References — 107

FIGURES

Figure 2.1. Duration of school closures in weeks (including holidays) between February and end-June 2020: OECD countries — 17
Figure 2.2. Distribution of hours of assistance by parents: France and United Kingdom — 29
Figure 3.1. United States: Employed persons who teleworked or worked at home for pay at any time in the last 4 weeks because of the Coronavirus pandemic by occupation (all adults) and by educational attainment (adults aged 25 years and over) (%), May 2020 — 44
Figure 3.2. Reported change in financial situation during lockdown: Australia, France and Switzerland — 47
Figure 3.3. Proportion of total population aged 16 years and over and of parents with children aged 16 years or less experiencing high anxiety — 51
Figure 3.4. Parents' relationship with children during confinement compared to before: France and United Kingdom — 52
Figure 4.1. Likelihood of a mental disorder, 5-16 year-olds, England, 2017 and July 2020 (%) — 65
Figure 4.2. Incidence of mental and social health problems in children (8-18 years) and adolescents before and during the COVID-19 lockdown: the Netherlands — 66
Figure 4.3. Opinions of parents regarding the instructional activities offered to their children by teachers, by child's level of schooling: France (%) — 69
Figure 4.4. Level of satisfaction of parents of K-12 children with the way children's school has been handling instruction during the school closure: United States, April 2020 — 69
Figure 4.5. Parents' views of the impact of enforced school closures on children's learning by level of schooling: Ireland, August 2020 — 70
Figure 4.6. Parents' views regarding the likelihood that the COVID-19 pandemic will lead to their child not making as much progress academically (% by category), United States, May 2020 — 71
Figure 4.7. Mean scores in reading and mathematics: Year 5 pupils, Baden-Württemberg, 2015-2020 — 76
Figure 4.8. Proportion of Year 6 pupils with satisfactory or better mastery of French and Mathematics: France, 2017-2020 — 76

TABLES

Table 2.1. Mode of delivery of lessons, learning resources, schoolwork during school closures – Czech Republic, France, Germany, United Kingdom and the United States: March-June 2020 — 20
Table 2.2. Access to digital learning resources (equipment and connectivity): March-June 2020 — 22
Table 2.3. Distribution and average time per day devoted to schoolwork during school closures: France, Germany, Ireland and the United Kingdom — 25
Table 2.4. Average hours in the previous week spent on different schooling learning/teaching activities, households and individual pupils: United States — 25
Table 2.5. Hours of schoolwork by parents' level of education — 26

Table 2.6. Proportion of parents providing assistance for their child's schooling: France, United Kingdom, United States	28
Table 2.7. Distribution of hours of assistance by parents: France and United Kingdom	29
Table 2.8. The relationship between parental socio-economic status and the provision of assistance by parents: France, Germany, the United Kingdom and the United States	30
Table 2.9. Children's difficulties with remote learning	33
Table 3.1. Incidence of temporary inactivity: Australia, France, Ireland, United Kingdom and United States	42
Table 3.2. Incidence of homeworking or teleworking	43
Table 3.3. Reported change in financial situation during lockdown: Australia, France and Switzerland (%)	46
Table 3.4. COVID-19 among household members and relatives, colleagues and friends: France and Switzerland	48
Table 3.5. Psychological well-being: prior to, at the start of and following lockdowns in March-June 2020	50
Table 4.1. Parents' views regarding their children's schooling and educational progress during lockdowns	67
Table 4.2. The relationship between socio-economic background and parental concerns regarding the academic progress of children	72
Table 4.3. Methodological features of comparisons of the academic performance of COVID cohorts with pre-COVID cohorts	78
Table 4.4. Academic performance of COVID cohorts compared to peers in previous years	80
Table A A.1. Main survey data sources	101
Table A B.1. Lockdown measures: February-June 2020 – Selected countries	105

Executive summary

The lockdowns put in place to control the spread of the COVID-19 virus during the period March-June 2020 represented a sudden, dramatic and unexpected disruption to all components of social and economic life which affected the lives of children and their families and transformed the educational experience of children over a period of 2-3 months and, sometimes, more.

School systems had to rapidly improvise to ensure some continuity in the education of children and adapt their teaching methods to a situation in which, in the space of a day, education moved from the school to the home for most children and the mode of instruction shifted from face-to-face contact to remote learning.

The home and social environment of children was also affected in many ways, which, in their turn, affected the educational experience of children. In-person contact with people other than household members was severely restricted. The working arrangements of many parents changed, often dramatically. Many were laid-off on a temporary basis or had to work from home. In addition, parents faced a range of stresses associated with the pandemic: concerns for the health of themselves, family and friends, financial worries related to changed working arrangements, reduced interactions with friends, relatives and family, and the demands of home-based schooling and childcare.

This report offers an initial overview of the circumstances, nature and outcomes of the education of schoolchildren during the first wave of COVID-19 lockdowns. Its purpose is primarily descriptive: it presents information from high quality quantitative studies on the experience of learning during this period in order to ground the discussion of these issues in empirical examples.

Three interrelated topics are covered: the nature of the educational experience during lockdowns; the home environment; and the mental health and learning outcomes for children during this period. The data come primarily from 5 countries (France, Germany, Ireland, the United Kingdom and the United States) with additional information on some aspects for 6 additional countries (Australia, Belgium [Flanders], Canada, Finland, Italy and the Netherlands).

Schooling during lockdowns

The duration of school closures was between 0-19 weeks in OECD countries depending on the country and the level of schooling. Net of school holidays, closures meant the substitution of 4-9 weeks of face-to-face instruction with home-based learning in the majority of OECD countries.

Online tools and platforms represented the predominant modes of delivery of lessons and instructional material for students as well as for communication between teachers and students. Hardcopy or paper-based materials continued to be used. The use of live online classes or interactions with teachers was rather limited. Teachers may have placed more emphasis on preserving pupils' link with learning and reviewing content already covered earlier in the year than following the planned curriculum and introducing new content.

The time spent on schoolwork by children was about half of what they would have spent in classroom-based instruction in normal times and 10 to 20% of pupils may have undertaken no schoolwork at all.

Parents played an important role in supporting and supervising their children's education, particularly in the case of younger children. The average amount of time devoted by parents to supporting and supervising schoolwork was of relatively short duration and more time was spent on assisting younger than older children. While many parents felt comfortable in supporting their children's education at home, a large proportion did not – at least half, if not more, in the countries in which information is available.

Difficulties faced by children regarding education were of a psychological and social nature such as lack of motivation, loneliness, etc. Difficulties related to access to the technology needed to communicate digitally with schools and teachers and access to online educational resources were experienced by a significant minority of children even if most children in the countries for which data are available had access to Internet connections and the necessary devices to continue their schooling online.

The home environment

The period of confinement was a period of stress for many parents and adults more generally. The levels of anxiety experienced by adults increased considerably at the start of lockdowns and remained above pre-lockdown levels even after lockdowns had ended. Lockdowns and homeschooling created some conflicts and tensions in some households but, overall, the appreciation of the effect of lockdowns on family life was positive and relationships between parents and children were not unduly affected.

The chances of children either having contracted the COVID-19 virus themselves or living in a household in which their parents/guardians or siblings had been infected were generally low.

The proportion of adults working from home increased significantly and a considerable proportion of employed adults were temporarily inactive due to business closures or reductions in activity or lost their jobs. Financial stress was experienced by a minority of families, possibly reflecting the fact that considerable public support was available for both inactive workers and the unemployed in the countries for which data are available.

Many parents needed to reduce their working hours to accommodate the presence of children at home. Overall, most parents were able to manage to balance the competing demands of work and the care of and support for their children.

Outcomes

The psychological well-being of most children did not decline to any great extent during lockdown compared to the situation prior to lockdown. The proportion of school-age children experiencing serious or severe symptoms of mental or psychological disorders may have risen. However, the majority of school-age children, both before and during the period of lockdowns, did not display such symptoms.

Parents offer a mixed evaluation of the impact of lockdowns and school closures on children's development and learning. High levels of appreciation of the work of schools and teachers during school closures was accompanied by concerns regarding the effects of lockdowns and school closures on children's educational and social development. Many parents were concerned about lack of progress in some subjects and the possibility that their children were falling behind.

There is limited and conflicting evidence from standardised tests regarding students' learning progress during school closures compared to progress in "normal" conditions. The quality of the data varies somewhat, and the differences observed between the performance of students tested in 2020 or in early 2021 with students in the same year of school in previous years range from small increases to large falls.

At the very least, the available evidence suggests that it should not be automatically assumed that the school closures of March-June 2020 had a large negative impact on student progress and achievement.

The impact of social background

There is little doubt that the negative impact of the pandemic has been greater among disadvantaged populations.

Rates of infection and COVID-19-related deaths were higher in areas of low as opposed to high socio-economic status in England and France and among certain ethnic groups. At the same time, infection rates were positively related to education and higher among people at the top and bottom of the income distribution than in the middle.

Children from less advantaged socio-economic backgrounds had greater difficulties than other children with access to the devices and connectivity necessary to continue their education at home. Students who dropped out of education during the period of lockdown appear more likely to come disproportionately from disadvantaged backgrounds and to have had a prior history of difficulties with schooling.

In the countries covered, there is little evidence of the socio-economic status of parents having an impact on the amount of time children spent on schoolwork or the amount of time parents spent assisting children: children from all backgrounds seem to have devoted more or less the same time to their schoolwork and to have received the same amount of parental assistance.

The evidence regarding the evolution of achievement gaps between children from different social backgrounds affected by lockdowns and school closures in 2020 compared to their peers in previous years is mixed. Both little change in the size of achievement gaps related to social background and significant growth have been found.

1 Introduction

This introduction presents the objectives, methodology and data sources of the report. The report provides an initial overview of the available information regarding the circumstances, nature and outcomes of the education of schoolchildren during the first wave of COVID-19 lockdowns of March-April 2020. Its purpose is primarily descriptive: it presents information from high quality quantitative studies on the experience of learning during this period in order to ground the examination and discussion of these issues in empirical examples.

Schooling during a pandemic: An initial overview

The lockdowns put in place to control the spread of the COVID-19 virus during the period March-June 2020 represented a sudden, dramatic and unexpected disruption to all components of social and economic life. The combination of the closure of schools and the broader lockdown/confinement measures such as the restrictions on movement and the administrative closure of many businesses and other organisations affected the life of children and their families. It transformed the educational experience of children over a period of 2-3 months and, sometimes, more.

School systems had to rapidly improvise to ensure some continuity in the education of children and adapt their teaching methods to a situation in which, in the space of a day, the setting in which education took place moved from the school to the home for most children and the mode of instruction shifted from face-to-face contact between pupils and their teachers/instructors to some form of remote or distance learning, often supervised by parents.

The home and social environment of children was also affected in many ways, which, in their turn, affected the educational experience of children. In-person contact with people other than household members was severely restricted. The working arrangements of many parents changed, often dramatically. Many were laid-off on a temporary basis or had to work from home. In addition, parents faced a range of stresses associated with the pandemic: concerns for friends, relatives and family who were sick, fear that they themselves, their children, members of their wider family and friends would catch the virus, financial worries associated with job losses, business closures and temporary lay-offs, frustrations about reduced interactions with friends, relatives and family, reduced freedom of movement, etc.

This report offers an initial overview of the available information regarding the circumstances, nature and outcomes of the education of schoolchildren during the first wave of COVID-19 lockdowns of March-April 2020. Its purpose is primarily descriptive: it presents information from high quality quantitative studies on the experience of learning during this period in order to ground the examination and discussion of these issues in empirical examples.

Information on the response of education systems to the COVID-19 pandemic in different countries is available in a number of publications [see OECD (2021[1]; 2020[2]; UNESCO, UNICEF and the World Bank, 2020[3])]. The approach taken here complements the picture described by these studies. Its focus is the circumstances and experience of the education of children rather than the actions taken and policies implemented by educational systems at the various stages of the crisis.

Information is presented on three interrelated topics. Chapter 2 covers the nature of the educational experience during the period of lockdowns and school closures. Chapter 3 provides information on the home environment (the setting in which education took place for the vast majority of school age children) and Chapter 4 presents information on the mental health and learning outcomes for children during this period. Finally, Chapter 5 offers a summary and some concluding comments.

Data sources

Much of the information available regarding the activities, behaviour and opinions of the students, their parents and teachers (together with that of the general population) during the first wave of lockdowns comes from surveys that use non-probability sampling designs, most often volunteer samples[1] or quota samples.[2] The reasons for this are understandable: a perceived need to gain information quickly (Huber and Helm, 2020[4]) and the absence of easily accessible sample frames covering the target populations of interest. Such approaches do not provide a secure basis for making valid inferences about the populations and groups of interest from the responses collected.[3]

In contrast, this report draws on a corpus of information that is restricted to studies that meet a minimum standard of statistical quality. For survey-based studies, the requirement is that they based on *probability-based* samples – that is, from surveys designed to be representative of clearly defined target populations (e.g. the adult population, school students, parents of school age children, etc.). The statistics are thus based on samples in which each member of the target population has a known and non-zero probability of selection. The corpus of studies meeting this condition is small: they were published in English, Finnish, French, German and Italian. In May 2021, all OECD member countries were invited to provide additional studies meeting these conditions that could cast light on the different sections highlighted in the report, whatever their language of publication. Table 4.3 and Annex A contain the details of the main studies from which information has been taken.

The principal source of the information is surveys that have collected information regarding topics related to the experience of schooling during the first wave of COVID-19 lockdowns – i.e. during the period March-June 2020. For the most part, the respondents are adults, either the parents/guardians of school age children, an adult resident in a sampled household or, where relevant, teachers. Few surveys collected information directly from children.

The data come primarily from 10 countries: Australia, Belgium (Flanders), Canada, France, Germany, Ireland, Italy, the Netherlands, the United Kingdom and the United States. This reflects the (unfortunate) reality that high quality data on the educational experience of schoolchildren and the life circumstances of these children and their families during lockdowns were collected in a small number of countries.

The studies relied on in this paper also have their limitations, but of a different nature from those based on "convenience" samples. The need to rely on telephone interviews and web-based surveys (in-person interviews being impossible) meant that coverage of the target populations was sometimes reduced (not all members of certain target populations will have Internet access or a known phone number) and response rates were often low. In some cases, sample sizes were small. In others, experimental designs were used. An example is the US Census Bureau's Household Pulse survey which was based on a design that involved very large samples and assumed very low response rates. While all studies retained in the report were designed to be representative of some population, and thus provide more reliable information than "convenience" surveys, the error associated with lower than usual response rates should be taken into account when interpreting results.

References

Huber, S. and C. Helm (2020), "COVID-19 and schooling: Evaluation, assessment and accountability in times of crises—reacting quickly to explore key issues for policy, practice and research with the school barometer", *Educational Assessment, Evaluation and Accountability*, Vol. 32/2, pp. 237-270, http://dx.doi.org/10.1007/s11092-020-09322-y. [4]

OECD (2021), *The State of School Education: One Year into the COVID Pandemic*, https://doi.org/10.1787/201dde84-en. [1]

OECD (2020), *"Schooling disrupted, schooling rethought: How the Covid-19 pandemic is changing education", OECD Policy Responses to Coronavirus (COVID-19)*, OECD Publishing, Paris, https://doi.org/10.1787/68b11faf-en. [2]

UNESCO, UNICEF and the World Bank (2020), *What have we learnt? Overview of findings from a survey of ministries of education on national responses to COVID-19*, UNESCO, UNICEF, World Bank, Paris, New York, Washington DC., http://uis.unesco.org/sites/default/files/documents/national-education-responses-to-covid-19-web-final_en_0.pdf [3]

Notes

[1] A common approach is the use of "participative" or open access on-line surveys in which a survey form is made available via a website for any interested person to complete. Alternatively, an invitation is sent to a contact person who, in addition to being asked to complete the survey, is asked to pass on the invitation to others (e.g. other teachers in their school).

[2] A form of non-probability sampling in which targets are defined for the numbers of respondents with particular characteristics such as sex, age and educational attainment.

[3] While some studies weight respondents to known population totals, these types of approach cannot compensate for response bias due to the self-selection of respondents and ensure the representativeness of samples.

2 Aspects of schooling during lockdowns

This chapter presents information regarding the educational experience of schoolchildren during the school closures of March-June 2020. The source of information is primarily surveys of the parents of schoolchildren, supplemented with information from surveys of the pupils, teachers and other school staff and administrative data. The topics covered are: the setting of schooling; the mode of delivery of instruction; time spent on learning; support available from parents and others; challenges faced by children.

Two months of home-based schooling

In most, though not all, countries across the world, the measures implemented to control the spread of the COVID-19 virus during the "first wave" of the pandemic from late February to June 2020 involved generalised "lockdowns" – restrictions on movement and the size of gatherings (public and private), the closure of a range of businesses and other institutions including schools and other educational institutions such as vocational colleges and universities. The duration of school closures over the period February to end-June 2020 (the end of the school year in the northern hemisphere) was between 0-19 weeks (including vacations) in OECD countries depending on the level of schooling (Figure 2.1). Net of holidays in this period (school holidays plus other public holidays, amounting to around 2-3 weeks in most countries), closures meant the substitution of 4-9 weeks of face-to-face instruction with home-based learning in the majority of OECD countries. In those countries in which schools were re-opened for face-to-face instruction before the end of the 2019-20 school year, the reopening of schools was often staggered. Different year groups returned at different dates and pupils did not necessarily return on a full-time basis. In addition, some parents continued to keep their children at home even if they belonged to the age or year groups eligible to return to school. In some countries, schools continued to be closed from the end of July in the southern hemisphere or did not reopen at the start of the 2020-21 school year.

Figure 2.1. Duration of school closures in weeks (including holidays) between February and end-June 2020: OECD countries

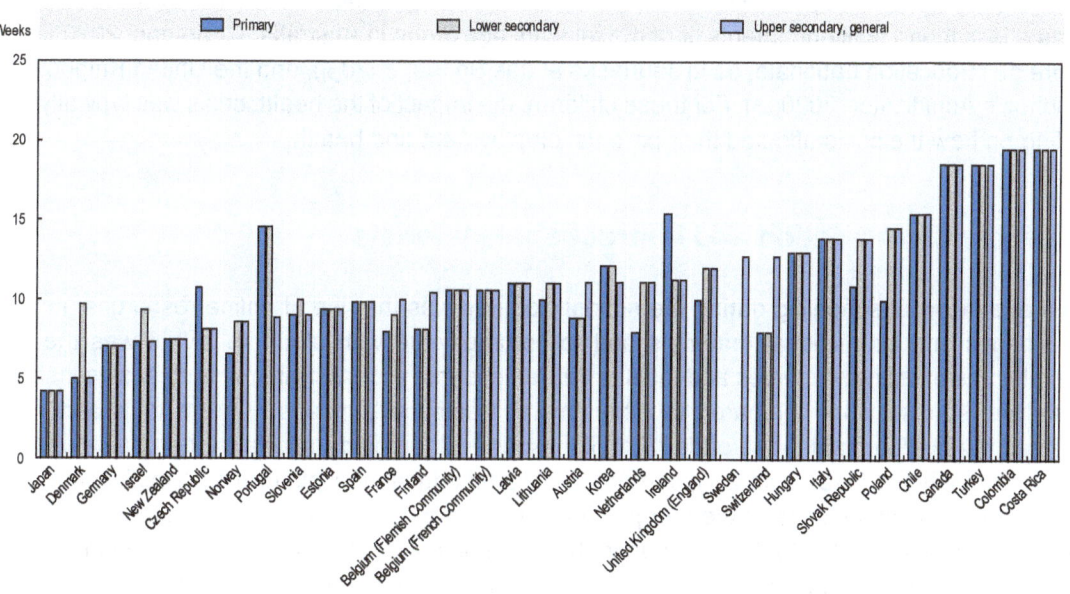

Note: Countries are ranked by ascending order of the duration of closures for upper secondary school (general).
Source: (OECD, 2021[1]).

StatLink https://stat.link/eqgrl3

The closure of schools did not mean that all children undertook their schooling at home. In some countries (including those covered in this chapter), the children of so-called "essential" workers or of parents who had difficulty looking after children at home during usual school hours as well as children in vulnerable circumstances could continue to attend school in-person. "Essential" workers covered a diverse group of occupations from high status health professionals to shop assistants and transportation workers. The available information suggests considerable variations between countries regarding the proportion of children that attended school in person during lockdowns. In England, the proportion of children attending school during lockdown was small. From the 20 March 2020 until the 1 June 2020 when schools started to reopen, between 1% to 3% of enrolled pupils attended school in-person on any day (Gov.uk, 2020[2]) with around 7% of parents in one study reporting that their child aged 5-16 years had attended school in-person during lockdown (NHS Digital, 2020[3], Table 4.1). In Australia,[1] in mid-May, 17% of parents/guardians reported that the child in their household attended school in person (Australian Bureau of Statistics (ABS), 2020[4], Table 3.1). In France, 31% of primary schools, 25% of lower secondary schools and 7% of upper secondary schools remained open for attendance by children of essential workers (Direction de l'évaluation de la prospective et de la performance (DEPP), 2020[5], Figure 7-1), but the numbers of students who attended are not available. In the United States, only 0.5% of parents reported that their child's or children's school remained open between April and June 2020 (US Census Bureau, 2020). In Finland, 5% of children overall continued to go to school, with big variations depending on the school level: in April 2020 (week 17), 1% to 4% of primary schoolchildren attended in-person classes, but the shares were much higher for kindergarten with 17% of attendance in person. In municipal and private early childhood and care institutions, in-presence attendance amounted to 27% and 32% of enrolments (Finnish Ministry of Education and Regional State Agency, 2020[6]).

In many countries, there was also a group of children whose mode of learning was not directly affected by school closures. These were children who were normally "home schooled". The share of such students among total enrolments is, of course, small. In the United States (where the phenomenon is the most widespread in the OECD area), for example, home schooled children represent around 3% of school enrolments (Snyder, de Brey and Dillow, 2019[7], Table 206.10).[2] Much lower shares are found in other countries – less than 1% of enrolments or of the relevant age group in Australia (Chapman, 2020[8]), France (Ministère de l'Éducation nationale, de la Jeunesse et des Sports, 2020[9]), and the United Kingdom (Office of the Schools Adjudicator, 2020[10]). For these children, the impact of the health crisis was typically indirect, depending on how the crisis affected their parents' employment and health.

The delivery of instruction and instructional materials

One of the features of schooling during the school closures was the use of online resources and tools to deliver lessons and instructional materials and to communicate with students. What was the balance between the use of online resources and tools to deliver lessons, access, transmit and receive instructional materials and student work compared to other, more "traditional", means? Online tools and platforms represented the predominant mode of delivery of lessons and learning materials for students undertaking their education at home (see Table 2.1), primarily dedicated educational platforms or applications or email. It is difficult to get a good picture of the part played by real-time online interaction with teachers during the period of school closures due to the variation in the questions and reference periods used in the different surveys. In France, 69% of secondary students reported that they attended remote lessons delivered by a teacher (or teachers) at some point during the March-June school closures (Direction de l'évaluation, de la prospective et de la performance (DEPP), 2020[11], Table 2) (though no information is available on the frequency or intensity of such lessons). In one survey in the United Kingdom, 25% of parents reported that their child had received real-time interactive learning in the previous seven days and, in another in England, 32% of parents reported that their child had received one or more online live lesson per day. Fourteen percent of German teachers stated that they had taught classes by video calls. In the United States, the average total time spent by all students in households in contact with teachers was 4 hours per week (see Table 2.5 below).

Paper materials provided by schools were also used by a reasonably sized minority of students, in most cases in conjunction with digital materials. In France 11% of secondary students received learning materials in the form of printed documents. In the United States, 19-21% of parents/guardians reported that their child's classes had moved to distance format using paper materials. Higher rates of usage of paper materials was reported in the United Kingdom where 34% of the children who were home schooled used some non-digital resources provided by their school. Teachers confirm this picture.

Several studies in Germany asked parents (or teachers) how instruction was delivered to school children (D21 Initiative/TUM/Kantar, 2020[12]; Huebener, Spieß and Zinn, 2020[13]; Vodafone Foundation, 2020[14]; Wößmann et al., 2020[15]). The overall picture is consistent between studies, despite differences in timing, questions and methodology. Table 2.1 shows two perspectives on this. According to parents, learning materials were predominantly accessed virtually (sent by email or the cloud mainly) or had been provided to students in paper form prior to schools closing, with instruction via videoconference being much less frequent. This is also in line with teachers' reports. Wößmann and his colleagues (Wößmann et al., 2020[15]) provide some further information (based on parents' reports) on the nature of the schoolwork children undertook during school closures. Students completed homework provided by schools (at least once of week according to 96% of households, including daily for 51%) and returned it to teachers (at least once a week for 78% and daily for 17%). Teachers gave feedback on the work (at least once a week according to 65%). Children were also often asked to read texts or watch learning videos (at least once a week for 73% and daily for 15%) and, to a lesser extent, use educational software/programmes (at least once a week for 57% and daily for 13%). All-class lessons via videoconference were relatively uncommon (at least once a week for 43% and never for 45%). One-on-one talks with teachers were even less so (at least once a week for 34% and never for 45%). In summary, most students were provided with homework digitally or in paper form, that they mainly had to complete by themselves and for which they received written feedback from teachers. The use of videoconferencing to conduct classes or to provide tutoring by teachers was relatively infrequent.

The extent of use of online tools and resources for the delivery of instruction and materials increased with the age of pupils and by level of education. The proportion of teachers in France suggesting activities to students that required use of a computer connected to the Internet was lowest at primary level and highest at upper-secondary level (see Table 2.1). In Germany, students in primary school were much less likely than secondary students to have contact via video conference or receive learning materials digitally, and much more likely to receive print materials before school closure. High school students in the academic track (Gymnasium) were also much more likely than other secondary school students to attend classes online via videoconference (Huebener, Spieß and Zinn, 2020[13]). In the United Kingdom, the proportion of children using school-provided real-time interactive online learning increased with the age of the oldest child and the use of school-provided non-digital resources declined (Office for National Statistics (ONS), 2020[16], Table 2). Similarly, the share of students having one or more online live lesson per day in the United Kingdom was higher for secondary students (36%) than for primary students (27%) (Benzeval et al., 2020[17]).

Some informant regarding the use of different modes of remote instruction by parental background is available for Germany and the United States. In Germany, the children of less educated parents appeared to have less interaction with teachers and less frequent use of most forms of learning platforms and materials during the period of closure than the children of more highly educated parents. Children from families with a parent with less than tertiary educational attainment were more likely to *never* have had a video-conference as a class (49% compared to 37% for their peers with tertiary educated parents); to *never* have had an individual discussion with a teacher (49% as opposed to 33%); to *never* have had a video to watch or text to read (21% compared to 10%); to *never* have had to use a learning software (34% compared to 26%); to *never* have had to submit homework (11% as opposed to 5%) and to *never* have received feedback on the submitted homework (19% compared to 10%). The likelihood that a student had never been asked to do some homework was, however, unrelated to parental education (Wößmann et al., 2020[15]).

Table 2.1. Mode of delivery of lessons, learning resources, schoolwork during school closures – Czech Republic, France, Germany, United Kingdom and the United States: March-June 2020

Country	Mode of delivery of lessons, learning resources, schoolwork	% of households or students	% of teachers
Czech Republic	Involved in online communication with their school (Basic schools grades 1-5)	89	
	Involved in online communication with their school (Basic schools grades 1-9)	84	
	Involved in online communication with their school (Upper secondary school, academic track)	96	
	Involved in online communication with their school (Upper secondary school, vocational track)	<80	
France	Often or always offering activities requiring a computer connected to the Internet (primary school teachers)[1]		67
	Often or always offering activities requiring a computer connected to the Internet (lower secondary school teachers)[1]		76-84*
	Often or always offering activities requiring a computer connected to the Internet (upper secondary school teachers)[1]		84-85*
	Received schoolwork via a digital work space or other educational software (lower and upper secondary students)[1]	95	
	Attended remote lessons delivered by a teacher or teachers (secondary school students)[2]	69	
	Received schoolwork via email or other discussion forums (secondary students)[1]	63	
	Accessed an online educational resource platform developed for use during the period of closures (secondary students)[1]	36	
	Received schoolwork via transmission of paper documents (secondary school-students)[1]	11	
	Received schoolwork via transmission of documents via telephone (secondary school students)[1]	11	
Germany	Teachers provided exercise sheets (primary and secondary)		84
	Teachers provided educational videos (primary and secondary)		39
	Teaching via video calls / conferences (primary and secondary)		14
	Learning resources are shared via email (primary and secondary)		69
	Learning resources are shared via a digital (learning) platform (primary and secondary)		41
	Learning resources are shared in the form of hardcopies via post or pickup (primary and secondary)		33
	Learning materials were accessed digitally (email, cloud) (primary and secondary)	86	
	Learning materials were handed before the school closures (primary and secondary)	52	
	E-learning with videoconference (primary and secondary)	27	
	Other mode of delivery of learning materials (primary and secondary)	14	
	Schools made no learning material available (primary and secondary)	2	
	Learning materials were accessed digitally (email, cloud) (primary and secondary)	86	
United Kingdom	School provided real-time interactive online learning[3]	25	
	School provided digital resources accessed via online learning platforms[3]	69	
	School provided digital online learning resources[3]	53	
	School provided non-digital resources[3]	34	
	One or more online live lesson per day[4]	32	
	Computer required for all school work[4]	49	
United States	Classes moved to distance format using online resources[5]	72-76	
	Classes moved to distance format using paper materials[5]	19-21	
	Materials provided online[6]		76
	Materials provided through a learning-management system[6]		83
	Materials provided in hardcopy[6]		56

* Depending on the type of school.
Sources: Czech Republic: (Czech School Inspectorate (CSI), 2020[18]); France: (1) (Direction de l'évaluation de la prospective et de la performance (DEPP), 2020[5], Figures 2-6 and 3-1) (2) (Direction de l'évaluation, de la prospective et de la performance (DEPP), 2020[11], Table 2); Germany: (Forsa, 2020[19]); (Huebener, Spieß and Zinn, 2020[13]); United Kingdom: (3) (Office for National Statistics (ONS), 2020[16], Table 2), (4) (Benzeval et al., 2020[17]); United States: (5) (United States Census Bureau, 2020[20], Education Table 2, Waves 1-6), (6) (Hamilton et al., 2020[21]).

In the United States, the proportion of households in which some or all of children's classes moved to a distance learning format using online resources increased with the educational attainment of the respondent and household income. It was also associated with ethnic background. Classes were more likely to have moved to online delivery among households in which the respondent was White or Asian (78% and 82% respectively) than Latino/Hispanic (72%) or Black (65%) (United States Census Bureau, 2020[20], Education Table 2).

The positive relationship between education and income and being a member of a black or Hispanic/Latino household and the probability of some or all of children's classes moving to online delivery may have reflected a deliberate choice on the part of their schools to use paper-based materials due to the difficulty (real or perceived) for their students to access materials online. The data suggest, however, that rather than compensate for difficulties with online access by using paper-based materials, schools may have chosen simply to cancel some classes. There were only small differences in the proportion of households in which some or all children's classes moved to a distance-learning format using paper materials sent home according to the characteristics of the respondent. However, children in low-educated and low-income household and children in Black and Hispanic/Latino households were more likely than children in more advantaged households to have some or all of their classes cancelled.

Access to digital devices and networks was limited for a sizeable minority of the population

Given the reliance on online delivery of instruction and learning materials and online communication between students and teachers, access to the necessary devices and networks was essential for students in order to continue their schooling successfully. What evidence is there regarding access to digital devices and the Internet during the period of school closures and the extent to which access was related to students' social background?

In many countries, a substantial minority of households and students experienced difficulties with access (Table 2.2). This is true even in countries where the level of access to digital devices and to the Internet is (almost) universal, as is the case in Germany (D21 Initiative/TUM/Kantar, 2020[12]) or in France (where 99% of students had some access to an Internet connection).

Unsurprisingly, access to digital devices and reliable Internet connections was related to social background. In France, secondary school students from advantaged social backgrounds were more likely than those from disadvantaged backgrounds to have access to devices such as a computer, tablet or printer/scanner (either belonging to the individual student or present in the household) (Direction de l'évaluation, de la prospective et de la performance (DEPP), 2020[22], Figure 2.2). In the United Kingdom, parents more often cited lack of devices as a reason for their children struggling to continue their education in low than high-income households. However, no clear relationship with level of parental education was observed (Office for National Statistics (ONS), 2020[16], Table 4). In the United States, the proportion of parents reporting that it was very or somewhat likely that their child would encounter at least one of three digital obstacles to doing their schoolwork at home ("needing to use a cell phone", "using a public Wi-Fi network because no reliable Internet at home" and "being unable to complete schoolwork because they did not have access to a computer at home") decreased as family income increased (Horowitz, 2020[23]). The share of households with children in public or private schools with a computer always available for educational purposes also increased with household income (United States Census Bureau, 2020[20], Education Table 3). Teachers in the United States working in high poverty schools were significantly more likely to report that their students lacked access to the Internet and devices at home (Stelitano et al., 2020[24]).

Table 2.2. Access to digital learning resources (equipment and connectivity): March-June 2020

	Proportion of households or students experiencing the problem
Australia	
No access to stable Internet connection	15%
Finland	
Not having adequate equipment at home (general upper secondary education)	4%
France	
Often or very often difficulties with connections or bugs (parents of lower and upper secondary school students)	25%
Access to a difficult Internet connection or no Internet connection (lower and upper secondary school students)	30%
Germany	
Problems with the Internet (speed, other)	31%
Too few or too old devices	14%
Ireland	
Adequate broadband not available	12%
Suitable devices not available	23%
United Kingdom	
Limited or no access to Internet	7%
United States	
Computer sometimes, rarely or never available for educational purposes	11-13%
Internet sometimes, rarely or never available for educational purposes	8-10%
Very or somewhat likely that child will have to use public Wi-Fi to finish homework because there is no reliable Internet connection at home	22%
Very or somewhat likely that child will not be able to complete schoolwork because they do not have access to a computer at home	21%

Sources: Australia: (Australian Bureau of Statistics (ABS), 2020[4], Table 3.1); Finland: (Finnish Education Evaluation Centre (FINEEC), 2020[25]); France: (Direction de l'évaluation de la prospective et de la performance (DEPP), 2020[5], Figures 2-4 and 3-3); Germany: (D21 Initiative/TUM/Kantar, 2020[12]); Ireland: (Central Statistics Office (CSO), 2020[26]); United Kingdom: (Office for National Statistics (ONS), 2020[16]); United States: (United States Census Bureau, 2020[20], Education Table 3), (Vogels, 2020[27]).

The school/school district played an important role in the provision of computers for use by students in the United States. Around 40% of parents/guardians reported that the child in their household had access to a computer provided by the children's school or school district for use outside school (United States Census Bureau, 2020[20], Education Table 4). The use of a computer supplied by the school or school district was highest among households headed by low educated and low-income adults and in households headed by blacks, Hispanics and Latinos. The importance of the school in the provision of devices in the United States is confirmed by a survey in late April/early May 2020 in which 78% of teachers indicated that their school provided students with devices (Stelitano et al., 2020[24]). In contrast, relatively low rates of access to devices provided by schools were reported in France and the United Kingdom. Some 8% of pupils in year 1 and 7% in year 9 in France used a computer or tablet provided by their school to undertake schoolwork during the period of school closures (Direction de l'évaluation, de la prospective et de la performance (DEPP), 2021[28]). In the United Kingdom, only 5% of parents who "home schooled" their eldest/only child indicated that their child used a device provided by the school (Office for National Statistics (ONS), 2020[16], Table 2).[3]

Teachers may have lowered their ambitions regarding the content of instruction

The closure of school buildings meant that the delivery of education had to be adjusted to allow (most) students to continue their education in their homes. In a number of countries, the content and focus of instruction and the amount of work pupils were expected to do was adjusted to reflect the new circumstances of learning. OECD (2021[1], Figure 1.4) reports that in 6 out of 33 countries for which data were available, governments gave priority to the teaching of certain areas of the curriculum or skills during the March-June 2020 period of school closures while, in a further 5 countries, decisions as to such adjustments were left to school districts or individual schools[4]. Surveys of teachers provide a more fine-grained picture of the adjustments to the curriculum and to the expectations regarding the content covered by instruction.

French teachers reported that the main priority of their school during the period of closure was to preserve their pupils' link with learning (53% of primary school and 58% of secondary school teachers) rather than to continue to advance with the teaching programme (cited by 5% of primary and 7% of secondary school teachers) or the consolidation of students' learning (cited by 23% of primary and 12% of secondary school teachers) (Direction de l'évaluation de la prospective et de la performance (DEPP), 2020[5], Figures 6-1 and 6-4). German and American teachers appear to have adjusted their expectations in similar ways. A survey carried out in April 2020 in Germany found that 35% of primary and secondary teachers aimed exclusively at maintaining the learning level of students before lockdown and that 45% expected to continue with the curriculum, but a slower pace than usual, with only 7% expecting to continue at the same pace as before (Vodafone Foundation, 2020[14]) In a survey of US teachers in late April/early May 2020, only 12% of teachers reported covering all, or nearly all, of the curriculum that they would have covered had their buildings remained open. In response to the question of whether they were focusing on reviewing content that was taught before COVID-19 versus presenting new content, 46% indicated that they were focusing mostly or exclusively on review rather than introducing new content (Hamilton, Kaufman and Diliberti, 2020[29]).

In summary, in the countries for which data are available, remote learning during the March-June 2020 period of school closures involved a combination use of online and paper-based materials, with more online delivery for older children. The combination of limitation in access to appropriate devices and connectivity, especially for lower socio-economic families, as well as reduced teacher ambitions about curriculum coverage hint to a reduced coverage of the usual curriculum during the month(s) of schooling at home.

Learning time during school closures

An important indicator of the effect of school closures and the associated changes to the mode of instruction on pupils' learning is the amount of time that school students devoted to educational activities during this period. This can be compared with normal instruction time at school to give an idea of the impact on the quantity of learning. While such comparisons are informative, some caution is advised in interpreting them. On the one hand, the estimates of student learning time at home reported by both parents and children are likely to be subject to reasonably large measurement errors. Parents may have an inexact understanding of how much time their children (especially older children) spent on schoolwork, and schoolchildren may over- or under-report for reasons of social desirability as well as difficulties with recall. On the other hand, official instruction time is not an error free measure of the time pupils actually devote to learning at school. Children attending classes are engaged in learning to varying degrees (from staring out the window to giving full attention to their lessons). In addition, in normal times, many students undertake some schoolwork at home in the form of own study, homework, preparation for exams and tests.[5]

Ten to 20% of students may have stopped their learning activities

One possible consequence of the physical closure of schools was that some children completely disengaged from school and spent no time on school learning at all. There are many factors that could lead to such a situation: limited supervision, support or encouragement provided by parents/guardians, failure of schools to provide schoolwork and instructional materials, teachers who lacked the experience or training to maintain the engagement of students through remote learning, lack of access to the technology necessary to maintain a link with their school and teachers (e.g. computers, stable Internet connections), living conditions that made study difficult or impossible (e.g. crowded apartments, lack of space to study) or simply lack of interest or willingness on the part of the student.

There is evidence that a small, though by no means negligible, proportion of students stopped (school-related) learning activities during the period of school closures. One measure of this is the proportion of students with whom schools had no contact. In the Czech Republic, schools lost contact with over 20% of upper secondary students enrolled in the vocational track, and between 11% to 20% of students enrolled in primary and lower secondary education (Czech School Inspectorate (CSI), 2020[18]). Smaller proportions of children were "lost" to the system in France, where teachers estimated that they had lost contact with 6% of primary school students and 10% of secondary school students in their classes while schools were closed (Direction de l'évaluation de la prospective et de la performance (DEPP), 2020[5], Figures 1-9 and 1-10). In primary education, these were children who could not be contacted either directly or through their parents or who refused to participate in learning activities (Direction de l'évaluation de la prospective et de la performance (DEPP), 2020[5], Figures 1-11). In secondary education, according to chief education advisors, these students were essentially students who had a history of absenteeism, lack of motivation and major learning difficulties (Direction de l'évaluation de la prospective et de la performance (DEPP), 2020[5], Figures 1-12 to 1-14). In line with these estimates, 8% of parents of French secondary school students indicated that their child had not done any school work set by his/her teachers during the period of school closures (Direction de l'évaluation de la prospective et de la performance (DEPP), 2020[5], Figure 2-8). In Germany, in 15% of households with school age children, parents reported that no digital school lesson or exchange with teachers took place (D21 Initiative/TUM/Kantar, 2020[12]). In the United Kingdom, 17% of 16-18 year-olds in full-time education surveyed between 7 May and 7 June 2020 indicated that they had *not continued* with their education in the previous week[6] (Office for National Statistics (ONS), 2020[16], Table 5).

In addition, there were children who did not receive any schoolwork from their schools. In the United Kingdom, for example, around 10% of parents of schoolchildren reported that their child had not received schoolwork to complete at home in April 2020 (Eivers, Worth and Ghosh, 2020[30]). The proportion was highest for children in upper secondary schooling. Around 25% of the parents of children in Key Stages 4 and 5 (Years 10-12) indicated that their child received no schoolwork. For children preparing for exams (e.g. General Certificate of Secondary Education (GCSE) and A-levels), this may have reflected the fact that they had already covered the relevant curricula by the time schools had closed and that there was no need to undertake further study during a period normally devoted to exam revision. In other data from the United Kingdom, 25% of parents reported that the children who were educated at home had not undertaken activities using material provided by their school in the preceding week (Office for National Statistics (ONS), 2020[16], Table 2). It is not possible to determine whether this was because no schoolwork was provided or because children and/or their parents decided not to use it.

Students spent about half the usual time on school-related learning activities

The amount of time students spent on schoolwork during the period of school closures is a topic covered in a number of surveys. The data collected are not completely comparable, however, in terms of the definitions of schoolwork, the reference period (an average day, the previous week) or the exact populations covered. Table 2.3 presents broadly comparable estimates of daily hours spent on schooling activities for France, Germany, Ireland and the United Kingdom[7] during the March-June period of closures. Data from the United States are presented separately in Table 2.4.

Table 2.3. Distribution and average time per day devoted to schoolwork during school closures: France, Germany, Ireland and the United Kingdom

Country	Age/Level	Distribution of hours devoted to schoolwork per school day (% of students)				Average hours per day
		Less than 1 hour	1-less than 2	2-less than 4	4 or more	
France	Primary (Year 5)[1]	32	32	20	11	1.8*
	Lower secondary[2]	9	21	51	20	2.8*
	Upper secondary (general)[2]	11	21	46	23	2.8*
	Upper secondary (vocational)[2]	22	33	36	10	2.0*
Germany	Primary and secondary	14	23	36	27	3.6
United Kingdom	Primary	16	29	34	11	2.3
	Secondary	16	17	39	27	2.8
		1 or less hours	2 hours	3 hours	4 hours or more	
Ireland	Primary	25	42	23	11	1.9*
	Lower secondary	8	22	24	46	3.1*
	Upper secondary	11	13	22	54	3.6*

* Averages calculated by the authors in the cases of France and Ireland.
Sources: France: (1) (Direction de l'évaluation, de la prospective et de la performance (DEPP), 2021[28], Table 10) and (2) (Direction de l'évaluation de la prospective et de la performance (DEPP), 2020[5], Figure 5-1, the data refer to the percentage of parents); Germany: (Wößmann et al., 2020[15]); Ireland: (Central Statistics Office (CSO), 2020[26], Tables 2.3 and 2.6); United Kingdom: (Del Bono et al., 2021[31]).

Table 2.4 presents data on the time spent in school-related teaching and learning activities in the United States during school closures. The first column concerns *households* and the second, *individual* schoolchildren. The data concerning *households* in the United States are not directly comparable with the estimates relating to individual children in the United States or elsewhere as: (1) they represent the sum of the hours spent by all children *in the household* on learning activities and all hours spent by *all household members* on teaching activities with children and rather than hours spent in learning activities per individual child and (2) learning/teaching activities are not limited to those based on material or lessons provide by schools.

Table 2.4. Average hours in the previous week spent on different schooling learning/teaching activities, households and individual pupils: United States

	Average hours per household per week (April-June 2020)	Average hours per pupil (May 2020)
Total	23.2	n/a
Live contact with teachers	4.0	n/a
Online meetings involving interaction between teachers and students	n/a	6.1
Teaching activities by household members	11.3	n/a
Students' own activity	7.9	n/a

Note: "Live contact with teachers" and "Teaching activities by Household members" equals average for Waves 1-6 of the Household Pulse Survey. "Students own activity" is the estimate from Wave 6 only of the Household Pulse survey (United States Census Bureau, 2020[20]).
Sources: (United States Census Bureau, 2020[20], Education Table 1); (University of Southern California (USC), 2020[32]).

In France (primary level), Germany, Ireland, the United Kingdom and the United States, the school week generally involves around 4.5-6 hours of instruction per day (23-30 hours per week) depending on the country and the level of schooling [see for France, Ministère de l'Éducation nationale, de la Jeunesse et des Sports (2021[33]); for Ireland, Gov.ie (2019[34]); and for the United States, National Center for Education Statistics (NCES) (2018[35], Table 5.14)]. Thus, in the countries for which we have data, the average amount of time (per day or per week) that school pupils spent on schoolwork (however defined) during the period of school closures was less than the hours of instruction time that they would have received at school in "normal" conditions. In France, Germany, Ireland and the United Kingdom (unfortunately the US data do not lend themselves to such a calculation), this represents about half the usual instruction time (about 3 hours against the 5-6 hours of formal instruction per day depending on the level of schooling). As noted above, in "normal" conditions, most students would also spend some time undertaking schoolwork or study activities at home in addition to the time spent in classes at school. Taking into account total time spent on schoolwork at school and at home prior to the school closures, the average time spent on schoolwork by German school children fell from a total of 7.4 hours pre-closure to 3.6 hours during closures (Wößmann et al., 2020[15]).

As can be seen from Table 2.3 there was considerable variation in the time spent on schoolwork by individual children. In normal conditions, the time spent by pupils being instructed in classes will not vary greatly as this is set by the school timetable and the relevant regulations. Variation in the time devoted to schoolwork will be due largely to time spent on schoolwork at home by students (e.g. in the form of study, revision, homework, completion of assignments, etc.). In the period of school closures, time spent on schoolwork was to a greater or lesser extent determined by the students themselves and their parents as opposed to the "institutional constraints" of timetabled classes.

Time on schoolwork and social background are not clearly related

The time children spent on schoolwork during school closures shows no clear relationship with either the level of education of parents/guardians (Table 2.5), household income or ethnicity.

Table 2.5. Hours of schoolwork by parents' level of education

Education of parent/guardian	Germany	Ireland		United Kingdom		United States	
	Primary and secondary students Average hours per day	Primary students Average hours per day	Secondary students Average hours per day	Student[1] Hours per week on school materials	Student[2] % 1-2 hours or less per day	Live contact with school[3] Average household hours per week	Students' own learning[4] Average household hours per week
Low	3.5	2.1	3.0	12	38	4.0	7.1
Medium	(x)	2.3	2.8	16	37	4.1	8.1
High	3.8	2.1	3.2	13	34	4.3	8.9

Note: Low education = full secondary education or lower; medium education = post-secondary non-degree qualification; high education = university degree or higher. In Germany, "low education" = less than a university degree and "high education" = university degree or higher.
Sources: Germany: (Wößmann et al., 2020[15]); Ireland: (Central Statistics Office (CSO), 2020[26], Tables 2.3 and 2.6); United Kingdom: (1) (Office for National Statistics (ONS), 2020[16], Table 2) and (2) (Pensiero, Kelly and Bokhove, 2020[36]); United States: (United States Census Bureau, 2020[20], Education Table 1), (3) average over weeks 1 to 6 of the survey; (4) data from week 6 only.

Of the four countries for which data are available, no clear relationship between the time spent on schoolwork and the education level of parents/guardians is observed in Ireland or the United Kingdom. A positive relationship is observed in the United States and in Germany, though in the latter case, the relationship is very weak, as was also true before the pandemic (Wößmann et al., 2020[15]).

Data on hours of schoolwork during school closures are available by the respondent's income (United Kingdom), household income (United States), by ethnic background (United States) and by socio-economic status and the level of disadvantage of the school (France). Hours of schooling were highest for students with highest income parents group in the United Kingdom (Office for National Statistics (ONS), 2020[16], Table 2) and (Eivers, Worth and Ghosh, 2020[30]) but no association exists between household income or ethnicity and hours of schoolwork in the United States (United States Census Bureau, 2020[20], Education Table 1). The daily hours of schoolwork for secondary students increased with parental occupational status in France (Direction de l'évaluation, de la prospective et de la performance (DEPP), 2020[22], Figure 1.1) and were higher for primary school pupils in non-disadvantaged than disadvantaged schools (Direction de l'évaluation, de la prospective et de la performance (DEPP), 2021[28], Table 10).

Interestingly, in both France and Germany, large differences in the time devoted to schoolwork during closures were found according to students' academic performance (as assessed by their parents). In France, for example, 52% of secondary level students judged to have "excellent" academic performance studied for 3 hours or more per day as opposed to only 28% of those with "significant difficulties" (Direction de l'évaluation, de la prospective et de la performance (DEPP), 2020[11], Table 1). In Germany, students with lower grades reduced the time spent on school-related work during the period of closures compared to the pre-COVID situation by 4.1 hours per day compared to 3.7 hours for students with higher school grades (Wößmann et al., 2020[15]).

Parental and family involvement

Given the limited direct contact students had with teachers, parents and guardians had to take over much of the role of the supervision of their children's education (including instruction) during the period of school closures. In this section, the role of parents, guardians and other family members played in the education of children is explored. What proportion of parents assisted their children and how much time did they spend doing so? What assistance did they provide and how comfortable were they with supporting their children's education?

The assistance from parents decreased with children's age

Data on whether or not parents/guardians assisted their children with their schooling during lockdown are available for France (as reported by students), the United Kingdom and the United States (as reported by parents/guardians) (Table 2.6).

In all three countries for which data are presented, the proportion of children receiving assistance tended to decrease as their level of schooling increased. Higher proportions of parents/guardians provided assistance for their children enrolled in primary school than for those in secondary education in the United Kingdom and the United States. In France and the United Kingdom, students at lower secondary level received more assistance than those in senior secondary schooling. This is likely to reflect the greater autonomy and independence of older children and the lesser expertise of parents concerning the content of the curriculum in the later years of high school.

Considerable caution should be exercised in in comparing the proportions of pupils receiving assistance between countries (and within countries using different data sources) due to differences in the respondent populations (students compared to parents) and to differences in the questions asked.

Table 2.6. Proportion of parents providing assistance for their child's schooling: France, United Kingdom, United States

Country	Level of schooling/age of pupils	% of parents providing assistance to children	Data item
France	Lower Secondary	75	Parents reporting that they helped their child(ren) regularly or occasionally with schoolwork
	Upper Secondary (general)	45	
	Upper Secondary (vocational)	55	
United Kingdom	Total	87	Respondent home schooled his/her child/children due to the Coronavirus (COVID-19) outbreak in the previous seven days
	Child aged 5-10 years	96	
	Child aged 11-15 years	89	
	Child aged 16-18 years	65	
United States	Children in elementary school[1]	49	Respondent, spouse or partner provided educational activities to household members doing educational activities at home
	Children in middle/junior high school[1]	30	
	Children in high school[1]	18	
	Children in elementary, middle or high school[2]	91	Parents reporting that they (or another adult) provided additional instruction or resources to their children beyond what was provided by the school

Sources: France: (Direction de l'évaluation, de la prospective et de la performance (DEPP), 2020[11], Table 3); United Kingdom: (Office for National Statistics (ONS), 2020[16], Table 2); United States: (1) (University of Southern California (USC), 2020[32]); (2) (Horowitz, 2020[23]).

Assistance was also provided by other family or household members (e.g. siblings) as well as by parents. In France, 21% of lower secondary school students and 14% of upper secondary school students[8] reported being helped by family members other than their parents (Direction de l'évaluation de la prospective et de la performance (DEPP), 2020[5]) Figure 2-5). In the United States, parents reported that between 3%-5% of school children received assistance from other household members depending on the level of schooling of the child (University of Southern California (USC), 2020[32]).

The *average* time devoted by parents in the United Kingdom to assisting children during the period of school closures is estimated to have been 2 hours per day to primary school children and 0.9 hours per day to secondary students[9] (Pensiero, Kelly and Bokhove, 2020[36]). In Germany, parents spent on average 1.1 hours a day working with their school age children (Wößmann et al., 2020[15]). In the United States, the total average time devoted to teaching activities during school closures by parents/guardians was around 12 hours per week – per household rather than per parent (see Table 2.5 above).[10]

Table 2.7 presents data on the *distribution* of the time parents spent assisting children in France and the United Kingdom. Parents devoted more time to assisting younger children (in lower grades) than to older children (in higher grades). A large proportion of parents in both countries reported that they provided little support to children enrolled in general upper secondary education. Some 70% of the parents of students in upper secondary general education in France and 90% of the parents of students at upper secondary level in the United Kingdom assisted their children for less than 1 hour per day and in many cases much less. For example, 47% of parents of students in general upper secondary education assisted their child(ren) for less than 15 minutes per day (Direction de l'évaluation de la prospective et de la performance (DEPP), 2020[5], Figure 5-2).

Table 2.7. Distribution of hours of assistance by parents: France and United Kingdom

Country	Level	Average hours per day (% of parents)		
		Less than 1 hour	1- less 2 hours	2 hours or more
France	Lower Secondary	40%	24%	36%
	Upper Secondary (general)	70%	17%	12%
	Upper Secondary (vocational)	22%	33%	45%
United Kingdom	Primary	21%	34%	45%
	Lower Secondary	60%	26%	14%
	Upper Secondary	90%	8%	2%

Sources: France: (Direction de l'évaluation de la prospective et de la performance (DEPP), 2020[5], Figure 5-2); United Kingdom: (Benzeval et al., 2020[17]).

Figure 2.2. Distribution of hours of assistance by parents: France and United Kingdom

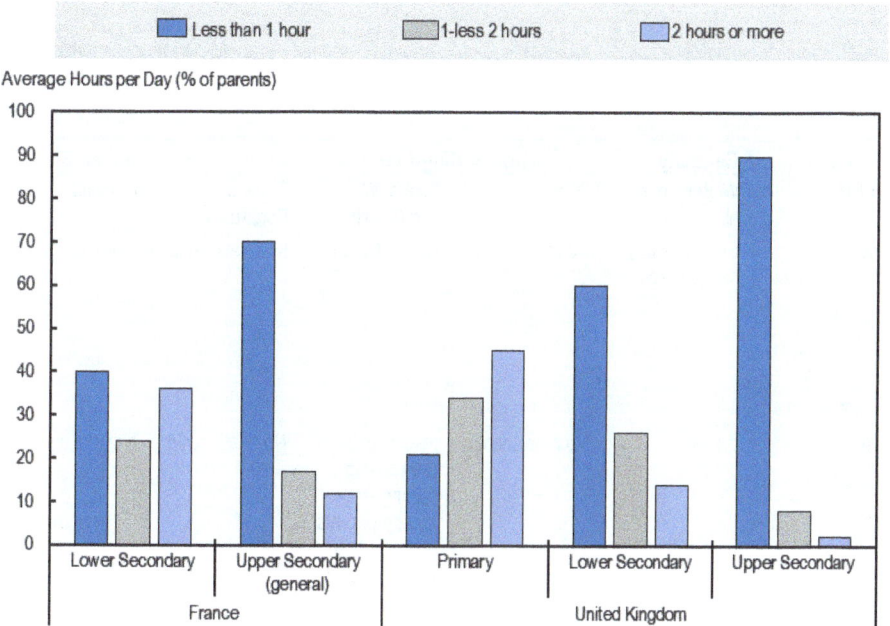

Sources: France: (Direction de l'évaluation de la prospective et de la performance (DEPP), 2020[5], Figure 5-2); United Kingdom: (Benzeval et al., 2020[17]).

StatLink https://stat.link/x6vkmf

Mothers tended to spend more time assisting their children with schoolwork during the period of closures than did fathers [see Benzeval et al. (2020[17]) for the United Kingdom, and Zinn, Kreyenfeld and Bayer (2020[37]) for Germany]. This is likely to reflect both the "typical" gender distribution of household labour as well as the impact of school closures and lockdowns (see below).

As expected, compared to "normal" times, the amount of time devoted to assisting children with schoolwork increased for most (but not all) parents during the period of school closures. Overall, 65% of the parents of French secondary school students said that they spent more time than usual during confinement helping their children with school work, 21% as much time as usual and 8% less time (Direction de l'évaluation de la prospective et de la performance (DEPP), 2020[5], Figure 5-5). In Germany, the average amount of time parents spent assisting children with schoolwork doubled from half an hour per day before the lockdown to 1.1 hours per day (Wößmann et al., 2020[15]). Similarly, in Italy, two-thirds (67%) of adults who cared for children of 0-14 years of age during lockdown reported spending more time in childcare activities (both homework and play) compared to an average pre-COVID day, 30% the same amount and 3% less time (Instituto Nazionale di Statistica (Istat), 2020[38], Figure 4). This was also true of parents in the United Kingdom who spent 40 minutes more on average on "developmental childcare" (which included assistance with schoolwork) in April 2020 than did parents in 2014-15 (Office for National Statistics (ONS), 2020[39]). Mothers increased the time spent assisting children with schoolwork more often than did fathers. For example, in France, 62% of the mothers of secondary school students reported increasing the time spent helping their children with schoolwork during the period of school closures compared to usual compared to 28% of fathers (Direction de l'évaluation, de la prospective et de la performance (DEPP), 2020[11], Figures 7 and 8). In Germany, mothers increased the time devoted to childcare (including assistance for schoolwork) during lockdown by 2.9 hours compared to 2.5 hours for fathers (Zinn, Kreyenfeld and Bayer, 2020[37]).

Regarding the relationship between parental socio-economic status and the provision of assistance by parents, the evidence is mixed and, sometimes, contradictory (Table 2.8).

Table 2.8. The relationship between parental socio-economic status and the provision of assistance by parents: France, Germany, the United Kingdom and the United States

	France	Germany	United Kingdom		United States		
Study	DEPP	Wößmann et al.	ONS	Eivers, Worth and Ghosh	Census Bureau	Horowitz	USC
Parental education	n/a	Small positive relationship	No relationship	No relationship	No relationship	n/a	Positive relationship (bachelor or higher compared to high school or lower)
Parental income	n/a	n/a	No relationship	Negative relationship (strongest among parents of secondary school pupils)	No relationship	No relationship	Positive relationship for elementary school pupils. No relationship for middle school pupils
Parental socio-economic status	Positive relationship	n/a	n/a	n/a	n/a	n/a	n/a
Data item	Secondary school student assisted by parents	Time spent by parents on assisting children	Child "home schooled"	Time spent by respondent or other family members actively helping student	Total time spent on teaching activities by household members	Additional instruction or resources to their children beyond what was provided by the school	Parent provided educational activities

Sources: France: (Direction de l'évaluation, de la prospective et de la performance (DEPP), 2020[11], Figure 3); Germany: (Wößmann et al., 2020[15]); United Kingdom: (Office for National Statistics (ONS), 2020[16], Table 2), (Eivers, Worth and Ghosh, 2020[30]); United States: (United States Census Bureau, 2020[20], Education Table 1), (Horowitz, 2020[23]; University of Southern California (USC), 2020[40]).

The lack of evidence of a consistent (and positive) relationship between parental socio-economic status and the provision of assistance to children in the countries covered is somewhat contrary to expectations. One reason for this may be that the circumstances of lockdowns meant that, during lockdowns, parents with low levels of education and income had more time available to assist children compared to parents with high levels of education and income than in normal circumstances. For example, employees in management and professional occupations – i.e. occupations associated with high levels of education and high incomes – were more likely than those in other occupational groups to continue to work paid hours as opposed to being in some form of inactivity (e.g. working zero hours, furlough, temporary layoff) during lockdowns (see Chapter 3).

The nature of the assistance provided by parents

There is very little consistent information across countries regarding the nature of parental assistance to schoolchildren. French parents reported that 57% of secondary school students were completely independent regarding the organisation of their work (and, therefore, presumably did not need or receive assistance), a figure in line with the share of students reporting receiving assistance from parents received cited above. Where assistance was provided, it consisted in providing help only when asked (37% of parents), checking completed work (37%) and working with their children (30%) (Direction de l'évaluation de la prospective et de la performance (DEPP), 2020[5], Figure 2-9). Over one in five parents (22%) reported that their child had undertaken schoolwork at their initiative (as opposed to work proposed by teachers or at the initiative of the child him- or herself) (Direction de l'évaluation de la prospective et de la performance (DEPP), 2020[5], Figure 2-8). From a different perspective, parents also assisted children by providing learning materials. Some 49% of UK parents who home-schooled their children reported that their child had used digital online learning resources and 40% that the child had used non-digital resources that they (the parent) had found (Office for National Statistics (ONS), 2020[16], Table 2). In the United States, in addition to using an online distance learning programme from their school for their child's education (70%), parents also used home schooling material that they had selected (26%), a free online learning programme not associated with their school (16%) and/or a formal paid learning programme not associated with their school (6%) (Brenan, 2020[41]). In Australia, 23% of parents whose children stayed home because of COVID-19 purchased additional equipment such as computers or desks to support their children's learning (Australian Bureau of Statistics (ABS), 2020[4], Table 4.1).

A US study looking at searches for online educational materials using the Google search engine (Bacher-Hicks, Goodman and Mulhern, 2021[42]) provides evidence in line with parental reports regarding their involvement in locating digital learning materials for their children. The intensity of searches for school-centred and parent-centred resources increased relatively to the same period in prior years with a peak in April from which point it declined but remained above previously observed levels. Demand for online resources increased in both high and low socio-economic status (SES) areas. However, the increase was substantially greater in high SES areas. Areas of the United States with higher income, greater Internet access, and fewer rural schools had substantially larger increases than did less advantaged areas.

About half of parents felt ill-prepared to assist with their children's remote education

Most parents assisted their children with their education during the period of school closures, even if the amount of time involved varied. To what extent were parents/guardians comfortable with, and prepared for, this role?

In both the United Kingdom and the United States, slightly less than half of the parents/guardians of schoolchildren appeared comfortable in their ability to support the home schooling of their children. At the end of April 2020, only 45% of parents/guardians in the United Kingdom agreed that they were confident in their abilities to support school work of their children within their household even if a much larger share (75%) believed that they had access to the resources they needed to help them "home school" their children/child well (Office for National Statistics (ONS), 2020[16], Table 1). Of parents who felt their child was struggling to continue his/her education, 36% cited limited subject knowledge on the part of parents/carers and 33% cited limited time (Office for National Statistics (ONS), 2020[16], Table 4). In a national survey of parents of K-12 students in the United States, 56% of parents reported that their child's remote learning had been difficult or very difficult for themselves and their spouse/partner (Jones, 2020[43]). Consistent with this, in May 2020, two-thirds (68%) of US parents reported that knowing how to teach children in ways they could learn had been a challenge in terms of the remote distance education of their child (Jones, 2020[44]).

Very similar results were found in France. Around half or more of French parents of secondary school students had some problems[11] finding the time to assist children (51%) and helping their children understand lessons (48%), with slightly lower proportions having at least some problems helping their child understand instructions from teachers (42%) or finding information about the schoolwork that needed to be completed (39%) (Direction de l'évaluation de la prospective et de la performance (DEPP), 2020[5], Figure 5-4). In another study, 35% of French adults with children reported difficulties in supervising their children's education (Albouy and Legleye, 2020[45]).

However, in Ireland, parents seemed even less confident (Central Statistics Office (CSO), 2020[26]). When asked in August 2020 whether they were concerned about their capacity to provide adequate home learning support if their child's primary school was closed in the new school year, 85% of Irish parents of primary school students indicated that had some concerns with 51% being very or extremely concerned.[12]

The relationship of parental socio-economic status with their perceptions of their ability to provide support for their children's education varies by country. In France, the proportion of parents in households with children aged 14 years or less reporting difficulties in ensuring the supervision of their children was higher among low income than among high-income parents (Albouy and Legleye, 2020[45]). In the United Kingdom, the extent to which parents were confident in their ability to support children in their remote schooling was unrelated to income (Office for National Statistics (ONS), 2020[16], Table 1). However, it was positively related to their level of education. Parents with higher degree qualifications in the United Kingdom were more likely than other parents to agree that they were confident in their abilities to "home school" the children/child within their household (Office for National Statistics (ONS), 2020[16], Table 1).

In Ireland, the reverse was found: parents with higher education qualifications were more likely to be "very" or "extremely" concerned about their ability to provide adequate home learning support if schools were closed in the new school year than parents with a highest qualification at secondary level or lower and less likely to be "not at all" concerned (Central Statistics Office (CSO), 2020[26]).

The challenges of home-based schooling for students

A number of surveys collected information on the difficulties or challenges experienced by school students in undertaking their schooling at home. As noted above, access to devices and networks represented a problem for some students. However, difficulties of a psychological and social nature seem to have affected more students than those related to access to and the use of technology (Table 2.9). The reported challenges for students were balanced by other positive features of home-based schooling and lockdowns (see, for example, the discussion of family relationships in Chapter 3 and the assessment of the positive and negative features of home learning and its impact on academic progress discussed in Chapter 4).

Table 2.9. Children's difficulties with remote learning

	Proportion of students experiencing the problem
Australia	
Difficulty concentrating	58%
Feeling lonely	49%
Feeling anxiety	33%
Finland	
Poor motivation to study (general upper secondary)	50%
Not enough support and guidance available	20%
France[1]	
Often or very often difficulties with motivation	37%
Often or very often difficulties with organisation of school work	19%
Often or very often difficulties with working autonomously	15%
United Kingdom	
Lack of motivation	40%[2]
United States	
Being separated from classmates and teachers is a major challenge	45%
Child's attention span or motivation is a major or minor challenge	44%

1. Students in secondary school.
2. Estimate adjusted to use whole population as denominator rather than only students struggling.
Sources: Australia: (Australian Bureau of Statistics (ABS), 2020[4], Table 3.2); Finland: (Finnish Education Evaluation Centre (FINEEC), 2020[25]); France: (Direction de l'évaluation de la prospective et de la performance (DEPP), 2020[5], Figure 2-4); United Kingdom: (Office for National Statistics (ONS), 2020[16]); United States: (Jones, 2020[44]).

Summary

The closure of schools as part of the lockdown measures implemented in the face of the COVID-19 pandemic in March-June 2020 radically altered the conditions and experience of schooling for pupils. Schooling moved from in-person to distance/remote instruction. In terms of the delivery of instruction and learning materials, the use of online tools and platforms predominated, with paper-based materials continuing to be used by a sizeable minority of students. Real-time interaction with teachers represented a relatively small component of the educational experience during the period of closures. While most pupils appeared to have access to the devices and networks needed to continue their schooling remotely, a significant minority (10%-30% depending on the country) experienced greater or lesser difficulties, with pupils from less advantaged families having greater problems than those from more advantaged families.

The average time spent on learning by school pupils during the period of closures was about half the usual or mandated hours of instruction. However, the ratio of the time spent on learning activities by pupils during closures to usual instruction time is a far from perfect measure of the levels of relative effort expended by pupils during closures and in normal conditions. Most, though by no means all parents provided support and assistance to children doing schoolwork at home and the majority of parents increased the amount of time devoted to assisting their children with schoolwork (and childcare more generally) during the period of closures compared to that provided in normal circumstances. Parental support was greatest for younger children in the earlier years of schooling. Across the countries for which data are available, no clear relationship exists between either parental education, income or broad socio-economic status and either the hours of study of pupils or the provision of support by parents.

References

Albouy, V. and S. Legleye (2020), "Conditions de vie pendant le confinement : des écarts selon le niveau de vie et la catégorie socioprofessionnelle", *Insee Focus n°197*, https://www.insee.fr/fr/statistiques/4513259#documentation. [45]

Australian Bureau of Statistics (ABS) (2020), *Household Impacts of COVID-19 Survey, Coronavirus impacts on job status, JobKeeper, superannuation, loan repayments, living arrangements, childcare, schooling and care provided. Reference period: 12-15 May 2020, Australia*, https://www.abs.gov.au/statistics/people/people-and-communities/household-impacts-covid-19-survey/12-15-may-2020. [4]

Bacher-Hicks, A., J. Goodman and C. Mulhern (2021), "Inequality in household adaptation to schooling shocks: Covid-induced online learning engagement in real time", *Journal of Public Economics*, Vol. 193, p. 104345, http://dx.doi.org/10.1016/j.jpubeco.2020.104345. [42]

Benzeval, M., M. Borkowska, J. Burton, TF. Crossley, L. Fumagalli, A. Jäckle, B. Rabe and B. Read (2020), *Understanding Society COVID-19 Survey April Briefing Note: Home schooling*, Institute for Social and Economic Research (ISER), University of Essex, https://www.understandingsociety.ac.uk/research/publications/526136. [17]

Brenan, M. (2020), *42% of Parents Worry COVID-19 Will Affect Child's Education, Gallup Panel, 24-29 March 2020*, https://news.gallup.com/poll/305819/parents-worry-covid-affect-child-education.aspx. [41]

Central Statistics Office (CSO) (2020), *Social Impact of COVID-19 Survey: The Reopening of Schools*, CSO statistical publication, 27 August 2020, Ireland, https://www.cso.ie/en/releasesandpublications/ep/p-sic19ros/socialimpactofcovid-19surveyaugust2020thereopeningofschools/. [26]

Chapman, S. (2020), *Australia Homeschooling Trends Over the Last Decade*, Home School Legal Defense Association (HSLDA), https://hslda.org/post/australia-homeschooling-trends-over-the-last-decade. [8]

Czech School Inspectorate (CSI) (2020), *Distance learning in basic and upper secondary schools in the Czech Republic, Thematic Report*, Česká školní inspekce, https://www.oecd.org/education/Czech-republic-distance-learning-in-secondary-schools.pdf. [18]

D21 Initiative/TUM/Kantar (2020), *Erfolgreiches Homeschooling während Corona*, https://www.kantar.com/de/inspiration/d21/erfolgreiches-homeschooling-waehrend-corona. [12]

Del Bono, E., L. Fumagalli, A. Holford and B. Rabe (2021), *Coping with school closures: changes in home-schooling during COVID-19*, Institute for Social and Economic Research (ISER) Report July 2021, University of Essex, https://www.iser.essex.ac.uk/files/news/2021/little-inequality-homeschool/coping-with-school-closures.pdf. [31]

Direction de l'évaluation, de la prospective et de la performance (DEPP) (2021), *Dispositif d'évaluation des conséquences de la crise sanitaire : comment les élèves ont-ils vécu le confinement de mars-avril 2020 ? Note d'information n°21.19 – Avril 2021*, Ministère de l'Education nationale, de la Jeunesse et des Sports, https://www.education.gouv.fr/dispositif-d-evaluation-des-consequences-de-la-crise-sanitaire-comment-les-eleves-ont-ils-vecu-le-322830. [28]

Direction de l'évaluation, de la prospective et de la performance (DEPP) (2020), *Confinement : un investissement scolaire important des élèves du second degré, essentiellement différencié selon leur niveau scolaire, Note d'information n°20.42*, Ministère de l'Éducation nationale, de la Jeunesse et des Sports, https://www.education.gouv.fr/confinement-un-investissement-scolaire-important-des-eleves-du-second-degre-essentiellement-307441. [11]

Direction de l'évaluation, de la prospective et de la performance (DEPP) (2020), *Pendant le confinement, c'est avant tout le niveau scolaire des élèves du second degré qui a pesé sur le vécu de la continuité pédagogique, document de travail n°2020-E06 – Décembre 2020*, Ministère de l'Éducation nationale, de la Jeunesse et des Sports, https://www.education.gouv.fr/pendant-le-confinement-c-est-avant-tout-le-niveau-scolaire-des-eleves-du-second-degre-qui-pese-sur-307632. [22]

Direction de l'évaluation de la prospective et de la performance (DEPP) (2020), *Continuité pédagogique - période de mars à mai 2020 - enquêtes de la DEPP auprès des familles et des personnels de l'Éducation nationale – premiers résultats, Document de travail n°2020-E03*, Ministère de l'Education nationale, de la Jeunesse et des Sports, https://www.education.gouv.fr/continuite-pedagogique-periode-de-mars-mai-2020-enquetes-de-la-depp-aupres-des-familles-et-des-305262. [5]

Eivers, E., J. Worth and A. Ghosh (2020), *Home learning during Covid-19: findings from the Understanding Society longitudinal study*, National Foundation for Educational Research (NFER), Slough, https://www.nfer.ac.uk/media/4101/home_learning_during_covid_19_findings_from_the_understanding_society_longitudinal_study.pdf. [30]

Finnish Education Evaluation Centre (FINEEC) (2020), *Exceptional teaching arrangements effects on equality and equity*, https://karvi.fi/en/2020/06/18/impacts-of-the-exceptional-teaching-arrangements-on-equity-challenges-include-distance-learning-skills-and-support-and-guidance-for-learning/. [25]

Finnish Ministry of Education and Regional State Agency (2020), *Municipal survey: support for learning and student welfare must also be invested in exceptional circumstances*, https://minedu.fi/-/kuntakysely-oppimisen-tukeen-ja-oppilashuoltoon-taytyy-panostaa-myos-poikkeusoloissa. [6]

Forsa (2020), *Das Deutsche Schulbarometer Spezial Corona-Krise: Ergebnisse einer Befragung von Lehrerinnen und Lehrern an allgemeinbildenden Schulen im Auftrag der Robert Bosch Stiftung in Kooperation mit der ZEIT, Lehrer-Umfrage - Erstmals repräsentative*, https://deutsches-schulportal.de/unterricht/das-deutsche-schulbarometer-spezial-corona-krise/. [19]

Gov.ie (2019), *Department of Education portal*, https://www.gov.ie/en/policy/655184-education/. [34]

Gov.uk (2020), *Attendance in education and early years settings during the coronavirus (COVID-19) outbreak, Week 33 2020 – Explore education statistics*, https://explore-education-statistics.service.gov.uk/find-statistics/attendance-in-education-and-early-years-settings-during-the-coronavirus-covid-19-outbreak/2020-week-33. [2]

Hamilton, L., D. Grant, J. Kaufman, M. Diliberti, H. Schwartz, G. Hunter, C. Setodji, and C. Young (2020), *COVID-19 and the State of K-12 Schools: Results and Technical Documentation from the Spring 2020 American Educator Panels COVID-19 Surveys*, RAND Corporation, http://dx.doi.org/10.7249/rra168-1. [21]

Hamilton, L., J. Kaufman and M. Diliberti (2020), *Teaching and Leading Through a Pandemic: Key Findings from the American Educator Panels Spring 2020 COVID-19 Surveys*, RAND Corporation, http://dx.doi.org/10.7249/rra168-2. [29]

Horowitz, J. (2020), *Lower-income parents most concerned about their children falling behind amid COVID-19 school closures, Fact Tank April 15, 2020*, Pew Research Centre, https://www.pewresearch.org/fact-tank/2020/04/15/lower-income-parents-most-concerned-about-their-children-falling-behind-amid-covid-19-school-closures/. [23]

Huebener, M., K. Spieß and S. Zinn (2020), *SchülerInnen in Corona-Zeiten: Teils deutliche Unterschiede im Zugang zu Lernmaterial nach Schultypen und -trägern*, Deutsches Institut für Wirtschaftsforschung (DIW) Wochenbericht n°47, https://doi.org/10.18723/diw_wb:2020-47-1. [13]

Instituto Nazionale di Statistica (Istat) (2020), *Fase 1: Le Giornate in Casa Durante il Lockdown: 5 Aprile – 21 Aprile 2020*, https://www.istat.it/it/files/2020/06/Giornate_in_casa_durante_lockdown.pdf. [38]

Jones, J. (2020), *Social Factors Most Challenging in COVID-19 Distance Learning, Gallup Panel, 11-24 May 2020*, https://news.gallup.com/poll/312566/social-factors-challenging-covid-distance-learning.aspx. [44]

Jones, J. (2020), *Amid School Closures, Children Feeling Happiness, Boredom, Gallup Panel, 25 May-8 June 2020*, https://news.gallup.com/poll/306140/amid-school-closures-children-feeling-happiness-boredom.aspx. [43]

Kunzman, R. and M. Gaither (2020), "Homeschooling: An updated comprehensive survey of the research", *Other Education: The Journal of Educational Alternatives*, Vol. 9/1, https://www.othereducation.org/index.php/OE/article/view/259. [46]

Ministère de l'Éducation nationale, de la Jeunesse et des Sports (2021), *Programmes et horaires à l'école élémentaire*, https://www.education.gouv.fr/programmes-et-horaires-l-ecole-elementaire-9011. [33]

Ministère de l'Éducation nationale, de la Jeunesse et des Sports (2020), *Projet de loi confortant le respect des principes de la République : quelles mesures pour l'éducation ?*, https://www.education.gouv.fr/projet-de-loi-confortant-le-respect-des-principes-de-la-republique-quelles-mesures-pour-l-education-307871. [9]

National Center for Education Statistics (NCES) (2018), *State Education Reforms (SER) - Table 5.14. Number of instructional days and hours in the school year, by state: 2018*, https://nces.ed.gov/programs/statereform/tab5_14.asp. [35]

NHS Digital (2020), *Mental Health of Children and Young People in England, 2020: Wave 1 follow up to the 2017 survey*, https://digital.nhs.uk/data-and-information/publications/statistical/mental-health-of-children-and-young-people-in-england/2020-wave-1-follow-up/data-sets. [3]

OECD (2021), *The State of School Education: One Year into the COVID Pandemic*, https://doi.org/10.1787/201dde84-en. [1]

Office for National Statistics (ONS) (2020), *Coronavirus and homeschooling in Great Britain: April to June 2020. Analysis of homeschooling in Great Britain during the coronavirus (COVID-19) pandemic from the Opinions and Lifestyle Survey*, https://www.ons.gov.uk/peoplepopulationandcommunity/educationandchildcare/articles/coronavirusandhomeschoolingingreatbritain/apriltojune2020. [16]

Office for National Statistics (ONS) (2020), *Parenting in lockdown: Coronavirus and the effects on work-life balance*, http://www.ons.gov.uk/peoplepopulationandcommunity/healthandsocialcare/conditionsanddiseases/articles/parentinginlockdowncoronavirusandtheeffectsonworklifebalance/2020-07-22. [39]

Office of the Schools Adjudicator (2020), *Office of the Schools Adjudicator Annual Report September 2018 to August 2019*, Department for Education Publishing service, https://assets.publishing.service.gov.uk/government/uploads/system/uploads/attachment_data/file/872007/OSA_Annual_Report_Sept_2018_to_Aug_2019_corrected.pdf. [10]

Pensiero, N., A. Kelly and C. Bokhove (2020), *Learning inequalities during the Covid-19 pandemic: how families cope with home-schooling*, University of Southampton, https://doi.org/10.5258/SOTON/P0025. [36]

Snyder, T., C. de Brey and S. Dillow (2019), *Digest of Education Statistics 2018 (NCES 2020-009)*, National Center for Education Statistics, Institute of Education Sciences, U.S. Department of Education, Washington, DC, https://nces.ed.gov/pubs2020/2020009.pdf. [7]

Stelitano, L., S. Doan, A. Woo, M. Diliberti, J. Kaufman and D. Henry (2020), *The Digital Divide and COVID-19: Teachers' Perceptions of Inequities in Students' Internet Access and Participation in Remote Learning*, RAND Corporation, http://dx.doi.org/10.7249/rra134-3. [24]

United States Census Bureau (2020), *Household Pulse Survey: Measuring Social and Economic Impacts during the Coronavirus Pandemic*, https://www.census.gov/programs-surveys/household-pulse-survey.html. [20]

University of Southern California (USC) (2020), *Understanding Coronavirus in America Tracking Survey – Methodology and Select Crosstab Results UAS 242*, Wave 4, April 29-May 26, 2020, University of Southern California, Dornsife Center for Economic and Social Research, https://uasdata.usc.edu/index.php. [40]

University of Southern California (USC) (2020), *Understanding Coronavirus in America, Methodology and Topline Results UAS 242*, Wave 4, April 29-May 26, 2020, University of Southern California, Dornsife Center for Economic and Social Research, https://uasdata.usc.edu/index.php. [32]

Vodafone Foundation (2020), *Schule auf Distanz: Perspektiven und Empfehlungen für den neuen Schulalltag Eine repräsentative Befragung von Lehrkräften in Deutschland*, https://www.vodafone-stiftung.de/wp-content/uploads/2020/05/Vodafone-Stiftung-Deutschland_Studie_Schule_auf_Distanz.pdf. [14]

Vogels, E. (2020), *59% of U.S. parents with lower incomes say their child may face digital obstacles in schoolwork*, Pew Research Center, https://www.pewresearch.org/fact-tank/2020/09/10/59-of-u-s-parents-with-lower-incomes-say-their-child-may-face-digital-obstacles-in-schoolwork/. [27]

Wößmann, L., V. Freundl, E. Grewenig, P. Lergetporer, K. Werner and L. Zierow (2020), "Bildung in der Coronakrise: Wie haben die Schulkinder die Zeit der Schulschließungen verbracht, und welche Bildungsmaßnahmen befürworten die Deutschen?", *ifo Schnelldienst*, Vol. 73/9, pp. 25-39, https://www.ifo.de/publikationen/2020/aufsatz-zeitschrift/bildung-der-coronakrise-wie-haben-die-schulkinder-die-zeit. [15]

Zinn, S., M. Kreyenfeld and M. Bayer (2020), *Kinderbetreuung in Corona-Zeiten: Mütter tragen die Hauptlast, aber Väter holen auf*, Deutsches Institut für Wirtschaftsforschung (DIW), https://www.diw.de/documents/publikationen/73/diw_01.c.794303.de/diw_aktuell_51.pdf. [37]

Notes

[1] Where less severe "lockdown" measures regarding restrictions on business activities were implemented than many other countries.

[2] In the US Household Pulse, around 5% of parents/guardians in the United States reported that their child was "already homeschooled" in waves 1-6 (United States Census Bureau, 2020[20], Table 1).

[3] OECD (2021[1], Figure 2.2) reports that over 80% of the countries providing data indicated that they offered support to "populations at risk of exclusion from distance education platforms" in the form of "subsidised devices for access (PCs or/and tablets)" during the first period of school closures. However, no information is available on what proportion of pupils had access to such support.

[4] In reality, what happened in practice was determined, to a considerable extent, by teachers. For example, most French teachers reported that they adjusted expectations regarding progress with the teaching programme during school closures even though reduction of curriculum content was not a formal governmental priority or requirement.

[5] In theory, the average time that children who are usually "home-schooled" (i.e. normally taught at home) spend on schoolwork may provide a more appropriate benchmark against which the impact of school closures on the time that children devoted to schoolwork can be assessed. However, little information is available about the time use of this (very small) group of students, who are, in addition, highly diverse in terms of family background and resources, the motivations for being home-schooled and the pedagogical practices of their tutors [see, for example, Kunzman and Gaither (2020[46])].

[6] The estimate is based on small numbers, however, and is associated with a large margin of error.

[7] Data on hours spent on schoolwork in the United Kingdom in the previous 7 days during May 2020 are also available from (Office for National Statistics (ONS), 2020[16]). Children aged 5-10 years spend 10 hours, children aged 11-15 years, 16 hours and children aged 16-18 spent 15 hours on schoolwork provided by their school. These data relate to the following population: parents/guardians in households with dependent children aged 5-18 years who a) indicated that they had home-schooled their child/children and b) indicated that the eldest or only child in the household being home-schooled had used resources provided by the school. This represents 66% of all parents/guardians with dependent school age children. As a result, the figures are likely to over-estimate the average time spent by all school pupils on schoolwork

as students whose parents have not supported their learning or received school-provided resources may have studied less.

[8] No difference between general and vocational tracks.

[9] The data is from the Understanding Society study. The question asked was: "How much time do you or other family members spend actively helping {childname}?"

[10] The US and UK estimates are not directly comparable as they do not refer to the same statistical unit. In the case of the US data, the unit concerned is the *household*. The UK data refer to individual parents.

[11] The proportions reported are those of parents reporting having problems "very often", "often" and "from time to time". The proportions of parents reporting these problems "very often" or "often" are lower.

[12] It should be noted that this question concerns the ability to provide home learning support in the future rather than a judgment regarding their current capacity as in the other studies.

3 Lockdowns and the home environment

School closures were implemented as an element of more general confinement or lockdown restrictions on movement and social contacts outside the household, administrative closures of business, requirements to work at home, loss of earned income, etc. Added to the risk of infection and uncertainty about the evolution of the pandemic, the situation created considerable stress for parents. What were the home conditions in which children lived and undertook their school activities during school closures? To what extent was the home environment conducive to study? This chapter explores four dimensions of the home situation: the employment arrangements and financial circumstances of parents; the health situation within the household; the psychological well-being of parents; and the relationships and interaction within families.

Introduction

School closures were implemented as an element of more general confinement or lockdown restrictions on movement and social contacts outside the household, administrative closures of business, requirements to work at home, loss of earned income, etc. Added to the risk of infection and uncertainty about the evolution of the pandemic, the situation created considerable stress for parents. What were the home conditions in which children lived and undertook their school activities during school closures? To what extent was the home environment conducive to study? This chapter explores four dimensions of the home situation: the employment arrangements and financial circumstances of parents; the health situation within the household; the psychological well-being of parents; and the relationships and interaction within families.

Employment and working arrangements of parents

The introduction of lockdowns in early 2020 had a considerable impact on the working lives of adults. In particular, a substantial share of adults who were in employment immediately prior to lockdown stopped working (they lost their jobs or were placed on temporary layoff or furlough) or, if they continued to work, worked fewer hours (in many cases zero hours) and/or worked from home. In this section, the evidence regarding loss of employment, change in hours of work, and change in the location of work among adults (including parents of school age children) during the lockdowns of March-June 2020 is examined. Annex B provides a summary of the restrictions related to employment and movement from home in the principal countries covered by this report over this period.

The changes to the employment situation and arrangements of parents flowing from lockdowns had an impact on the situation of children from several points of view. First, because they could not work or were required to work from home, a large share of working parents were present at home during lockdowns. This facilitated the task of caring for children and supporting their education at home for many, but not all, parents. Second, job loss and temporary layoff meant loss of income (even if this was offset by various forms of income support from governments) and psychological stress. Finally, the situation of those parents who continued to work at their normal place of work was complicated by the closure of schools and the need to organise childcare during school hours and support for their children's education (even if schools were open for the children of "essential workers"). For essential workers (essentially in the healthcare sector or in other occupations involving contact with the public), work involved a higher risk of infection for themselves and, as a consequence, their families.

Loss of employment

The scale of job losses during lockdowns depended to a considerable extent on the type of measures implemented to support workers and businesses affected by lockdowns in different countries. Most OECD countries adapted existing job retention/wage subsidy schemes to assist employers to retain employees on their payrolls during lockdowns and, in some cases introduced new schemes, thus limiting the numbers of workers losing their jobs (OECD, 2021[1]). A minority of countries chose to provide support primarily in the form of income support for workers who had lost their jobs or were on temporary layoff.

Unemployment rates remained relatively stable in the vast majority of OECD countries over the first half of 2020 despite the introduction of lockdowns (OECD.Stat, 2020[2]) with the exception of Canada, Colombia and the United States. The unemployment rate in Canada rose by over 5 percentage points from 7.8% to 13.1% between March and April 2020 and, in the United States, it rose by over 10 percentage points from 4.4% to 14.8% (OECD.Stat, 2020[2]). In both these countries, many workers who may have retained their jobs in other countries entered unemployment. For example, in May 2020, of the 42.5 million persons in the US labour force who were unable to work at some point in the previous four weeks due to the

Coronavirus pandemic, 31% were unemployed due to "temporary layoff" (Bureau of Labor Statistics (BLS), 2020[3], Table 5).

Hours of work

The hours of work of many employed adults changed dramatically following the introduction of lockdowns. In many OECD countries, working hours fell between 10% to 20% between March and April 2020 (OECD, 2021[1], Figure 1.9). The widespread use of job retention schemes meant that a large share of workers remained employed but worked zero paid hours (Table 3.1). For those who continued to work paid hours, hours of work fell (at the demand of employers or, alternatively, at the request of workers – e.g. to look after children or other family members) or, occasionally, increased.

Table 3.1. Incidence of temporary inactivity: Australia, France, Ireland, United Kingdom and United States

Country	Temporarily inactive (employed but worked zero hours)	Population	Reference period	Survey date
Australia	7-8%	Persons aged 18 and over	Previous 14 days	April 2020
France	37%	Employed Persons	Average week during confinement	Mid-March to mid-May 2020
Ireland	33%	Adults who indicated that COVID-19 had affected their work	Period of lockdown	8-23 May 2020
United Kingdom	30%	Employed adults	Previous 7 days	14-17 May 2020
United States	20%	Employed adults aged 16 years or over	Previous 4 weeks	May 2020

Sources: Australia: (Australian Bureau of Statistics (ABS), 2020[4]); France: (Jauneau and Vidalenc, 2020[5]); Ireland: (Central Statistical Office (CSO), 2020[6]); United Kingdom: (Office for National Statistics (ONS), 2020[7], Figure 4); United States: (Bureau of Labor Statistics (BLS), 2020[3], Table 7, May 2020).

The scale of the impact of lockdowns on temporary inactivity can be seen in data from France and the United Kingdom. In France, the share of employed persons who worked zero hours in an average week over the period mid-March to mid-May 2020 (37%) was 25 percentage points higher than that observed in the corresponding period in 2019[1] (12%) (Jauneau and Vidalenc, 2020[5]). Most of this increase was due to the increase of the proportion of workers in furlough ("chômage technique"). A similar impact is observed in the United Kingdom. At the end of March 2020 (immediately prior to the introduction of lockdown measures), only 6% of employed adults reported that they had not completed paid work in their job in the previous week. Two weeks later, this proportion had increased to 29% (an increase of 23 percentage points) and remained at this level into June (Office for National Statistics (ONS), 2020[7], Figure 4).

The incidence of temporary inactivity varied considerably across occupational categories. In particular, persons employed in managerial and professional occupations were much less likely to be in this situation than workers in other occupational groups [see, for France, Givord and Silhol (2020[8], Figure 2) and for the United States, Bureau of Labor Statistics (BLS) (2020[3], Table 7)].

For those employees who worked during confinement (i.e., excluding those who were temporarily inactive), some experienced changes to their hours of work. Of the 12% of Australian workers who indicated in mid-April that their job situation had changed in the previous two weeks, 51% stated that they were working fewer paid hours and 9% that they were working more hours (Australian Bureau of Statistics (ABS), 2020[9], Table 7.1). A month later, the shares of those workers whose job situation had changed who had increased (22%) or decreased (20%) their paid hours were much the same. In the United Kingdom, of the adults who indicated that COVID-19 had affected their work, 20% experienced a decrease in hours of work and 17% an increase. In the case of working parents with dependent children 17% saw a decrease in their hours of work and 15% an increase (Office for National Statistics (ONS), 2020[10]). In France, during the period of confinement (mid-March to mid-May), the working hours of employees who continued to work full-time decreased only by 4%, from 37 hours in 2019 to 35 hours (Jauneau and Vidalenc, 2020[5]).

Working from home

For employed persons who continued to work paid hours, widespread reliance on working from home or teleworking was a feature of the period of lockdowns. In many countries, nearly half the workforce worked from home or teleworked during the lockdowns of March-June 2020 (Table 3.2)[2].

Table 3.2. Incidence of homeworking or teleworking

Country	% working from home or teleworking at some point in the reference period		Population	Reference period	Date of survey
	Due to the Coronavirus	Any reason			
Australia		46	Employed adults working paid hours	Previous 14 days	29 April–4 May 2020
Finland		34	Employed adults	Previous 4 weeks	April 2020
France		47[a]	Employed adults	Previous 4 weeks	16 March–10 May 2020
		58[b]	Adults with job prior to confinement	Period of lockdown	2 May–2 June 2020
Ireland	45		Adults citing employment effects from COVID-19	Period of lockdown	8–23 April 2020
Switzerland	47		Employees and apprentices/interns	Period of lockdown	12 May–26 June 2020
United Kingdom		41	Employed adults	Previous 7 days	14–17 May 2020
United States	35		Employed adults (16 years and over)	Previous 4 weeks	May 2020

Note: Irish data refer to adults whose work was affected by COVID-19 and started to work remotely from home or increase their hours of remote work.
Sources: Australia: (Australian Bureau of Statistics (ABS), 2020[11], Table 2.1); France: (a) (Jauneau and Vidalenc, 2020[5]), (b) (Bajos et al., 2020[12]); Finland: Statistics Finland, Labor Force Survey cited by (Leskinen, 2020[13]); Ireland: (Central Statistical Office (CSO), 2020[6]); Switzerland: (Refle et al., 2020[14], Table 4.1); United Kingdom: (Office for National Statistics (ONS), 2020[15], 22 May 2020); United States: (Bureau of Labor Statistics (BLS), 2020[3], Table 1, May 2020).

As in the case of temporary inactivity, lockdowns were associated with a large increase in the proportion of workers who worked some or all of the time from home. The increase was less dramatic than in the case of temporary inactivity as many employees and self-employed persons already worked at home or had pre-existing teleworking arrangements. For example, in Australia, nearly one-third (32%) of the workforce reported regularly working from home in August 2019 (Australian Bureau of Statistics (ABS), 2019[16]). Similarly in France, the proportion of workers working from home increased from 23% to 47% between March-May 2019 and March-May 2020 (Jauneau and Vidalenc, 2020[5]). In the United Kingdom, the proportion of workers using their home as a place of work in April 2020 compared to before lockdown increased by 31 percentage points from 29% to 60% (Felstead and Reuschke, 2020[17]).[3] In Ireland, only 12% of adults who stated that their employment had been affected by COVID-19 indicate that their hours of telework had increased (Central Statistical Office (CSO), 2020[6]).

Many workers alternated home/telework with in-person presence at their workplace during lockdowns. In France, slightly over a third (36%) of employed persons who worked from home did so for less than a full week (Givord and Silhol, 2020[8]) as did 22% of workers in Switzerland (Refle et al., 2020[14]). In the United Kingdom, 8% of working adults worked both from home and from their workplace in the period 14-17 May (Office for National Statistics (ONS), 2020[15], Table 1).

The incidence of working at home/telework was closely related to the occupation of workers and, as a result, to their level of educational attainment (see Figure 3.1 for the United States). It was also related, though less strongly, to the presence of dependent children in the worker's household.

Figure 3.1. United States: Employed persons who teleworked or worked at home for pay at any time in the last 4 weeks because of the Coronavirus pandemic by occupation (all adults) and by educational attainment (adults aged 25 years and over) (%), May 2020

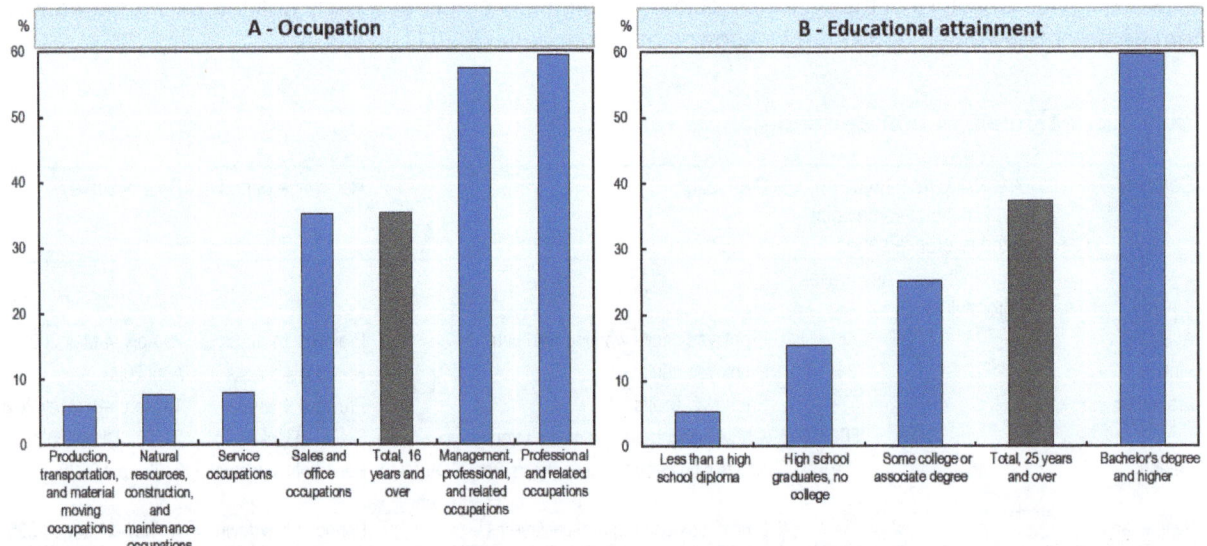

Note: Population for the occupational breakdown is persons aged 16 years and over and for the breakdown by educational attainment it is persons aged 25 years and older.
Source: (Bureau of Labor Statistics (BLS), 2020[3], Tables 1 and 2).

StatLink https://stat.link/rf4vgl

Workers in white-collar occupations (managers, professionals and associate professional, administrative jobs) were much more likely to work at home than other occupational groups. Employees in managerial/professional occupations had particularly high rates of home/teleworking – 80% in France, 83% in the United Kingdom and 59% in the United States by way of example. This compared to 6% of production workers ("ouvriers") in France, 21% of operatives in the United Kingdom and 6% of workers in production, transportation and material moving occupations in the United States (Jauneau and Vidalenc, 2020[5]; Felstead and Reuschke, 2020[17]; Bureau of Labor Statistics (BLS), 2020[3], Table 2, May 2020)[4].

Reflecting the distribution of qualifications by occupation, employees with tertiary educational attainment were much more likely to work at home than those with lower qualifications. Across a group of 11 OECD countries, the proportion of workers with college degrees working at home (55%) was on average 36 percentage points higher than the proportion of workers with no high school qualifications (19%) at mid-April or end-April/early May 2020 (OECD, 2021[1], Figure 5.16). Other surveys provide a similar picture. In Switzerland, the United Kingdom and the United States, the proportion of workers with a bachelor level qualification or higher who teleworked in May 2020 was 71%, 82%[5] and 60% respectively. In contrast, 26% and 20%-31% of workers with less than upper secondary education teleworked in Switzerland and the United Kingdom and only 5% in the United States (Refle et al., 2020[14]; Felstead and Reuschke, 2020[17]; Bureau of Labor Statistics (BLS), 2020[3], Table 1, May 2020).

The incidence of home/telework appears to have been slightly higher among adults with dependent children than among the rest of the population. In the United States in May 2020, nearly four out of ten (39%) employed adults with children 18 years or younger teleworked at some point in the previous

4 weeks. This was a slightly higher share than among adults without children of this age (34%) (Bureau of Labor Statistics (BLS), 2020[3], Table 1, May 2020). In Ireland, the incidence of telework was highest among 35-44 year-olds (an age at which family responsibilities are commonly high) (Central Statistical Office (CSO), 2020[6]). In the United Kingdom, workers working at least one hour a week in the week prior to the survey with children aged 5-15 years (65%) were more slightly likely to work at home than all workers (60%) (Felstead and Reuschke, 2020[17]).

School closures and the working arrangements of parents/guardians

A normal consequence of the closure of schools outside vacation periods is that parents have to find alternative arrangements for the care and supervision of their children as schooling takes place during the usual working hours of most workers. For working parents, one option is the re-organisation and, often, the reduction of hours of work (Viner et al., 2020[18]). How did school closures and the resulting need for parents to care for children and supervise their schooling during usual working hours affect the working arrangements of parents during lockdowns?

The impact of the closures in March-June 2020 on the working hours and organisation of working time of parents/guardians was moderated, to some extent, by the fact that many parents were at home due to the loss of their jobs, temporary inactivity or enforced home/telework associated with lockdowns. Nevertheless, balancing the demands of work and family responsibilities constituted a challenge for the parents of school age children who continued to work, especially mothers.[6] For parents in jobs that could not be performed at home (e.g. those working in sectors such as healthcare, retail sales, or transport) the issue was one of adjusting or reducing working hours (if possible) to fit in with parenting responsibilities or taking paid or unpaid leave. This was also true for some parents working at home, especially those who had limited autonomy regarding the organisation of their own working time during the day. Parents working at home who had the flexibility to organise their working hours to fit in with the presence of children at home also faced challenges. These included managing the lack of dividing lines between work, childcare/schooling and family life and the inevitable tensions generated in a situation in which family members were undertaking work and schooling under the same roof at the same time, often in close proximity.

An indication of the proportion of workers with dependent children who adapted their working arrangements to accommodate caring/schooling responsibilities is provided by surveys in Australia, Ireland, Switzerland, the United Kingdom and the United States. With the exception of Switzerland, a significant minority of workers in these countries, adjusted their working arrangements for this purpose. In Australia (Australian Bureau of Statistics (ABS), 2020[4], Table 4.1), 75% of parents with students or young children in their household surveyed in May 2020 reported that their children had stayed home because of COVID-19. Of these, 38% worked from home to care for children (suggesting that they had a choice regarding their working location), 22% reduced or changed their working hours and 13% took leave to care for children. Almost a quarter (24%) of persons aged 35-44 in Ireland reported having (unspecified) "childcare issues" in April 2020 (Central Statistical Office (CSO), 2020[6], Table 4d). As not all persons in this age group are parents, the proportion of *parents* in this situation will have been higher. Only 6% of Swiss workers who reported changes to their work situation due to lockdowns indicated that they worked less hours due to care duties (Refle et al., 2020[14]). In the United Kingdom (Office for National Statistics (ONS), 2020[10]), two-thirds (67%) of parents in employment who had at least one dependent child aged 5 to 18 years living in the household stated that the COVID-19 outbreak was affecting their work. Of these, 28% reported that they had to work around home schooling responsibilities with a further 3% reporting that they were unable to work at all due to home schooling responsibilities. The corresponding proportions regarding childcare responsibilities were 20% and 3%. In addition, 29% of employed adults who had home schooled their child/children in the previous week stated that home schooling was negatively affecting their job. In the United States, 20% of working-age adults said the reason they were not working was because COVID-19 disrupted their childcare arrangements (Heggeness and Fields, 2020[19]).[7] Similar conclusions were found in a study using data from the US Current Population Survey. School closures reduced weekly work hours among fathers and mothers of young school age children between 11% and 15% on average (Amuedo-Dorantes et al., 2020[20]). Overall, female parents were more likely than males to make adjustments to their working hours and arrangements [see, for example, Amuedo-Dorantes et al. (2020[20]) for the United States and Office for National Statistics (ONS) (2020[10]), for the United Kingdom)].

In terms of an overall appreciation of their situation, the available data suggest that the majority of parents who worked from home during lockdowns did not find balancing work and family responsibilities to be a major source of stress or problem, even if, in some countries, a significant minority experienced difficulties. Only 13%[8] of parents (with dependent children) in employment in May 2020 in the United Kingdom reported that they found working from home difficult (Office for National Statistics (ONS), 2020[10], Tables 6 and 8). In Ireland, 22% of working adults aged 35-44 years (the ages at which most commonly look after children) indicated that they had difficulties working with family around (Central Statistical Office (CSO), 2020[6]). Higher proportions of parents in Switzerland and the United States found balancing a job and family responsibilities during lockdown to be difficult. Around 40% of Swiss parents with a child under the age of 18 years (irrespective of whether they were in a couple or single parents) reported that it was harder to combine work and non-work life following the introduction of lockdown measures (Refle et al., 2020[14]). In the United States, 43% of US parents in employment felt that having to balance a job and helping kids with school was a major challenge (Jones, 2020[21]), and, 39% of adults in households affected by school closures agreed that school closures had made it difficult for them to work or do other household tasks (University of Southern California (USC), 2020[22]).

Financial stress

Reduced working hours, loss of employment, temporary lay-offs and temporary closures of businesses reduced income for those affected, even when there was substantial government assistance available. However, these effects were concentrated in a minority, even if a significant one, of the population. Overall, the majority of households did not experience negative consequences (at least in the short-term) on their finances as a consequence of the COVID-19 lockdowns.

Table 3.3 presents data from Australia, France and Switzerland from surveys using comparable questions regarding the reported impact of COVID-19 and the lockdowns on household finances.

Table 3.3. Reported change in financial situation during lockdown: Australia, France and Switzerland (%)

	Australia	France	Switzerland
Improved	14	2	11
No change	55	67	70
Deteriorated	31	23	19
Don't know	-	7	-
Population	Adults 18 years and older	Persons 15 years and older	Persons 15-99 years old
Reference period	Previous 4 weeks	Period of confinement	Period of lockdown
Date of collection	14-17 April 2020	May 2020	12 May–26 June 2020

Sources: Australia: (Australian Bureau of Statistics (ABS), 2020[9], Table 4.1); France: (Givord and Silhol, 2020[8], Complimentary Figure 1); Switzerland: (Refle et al., 2020[14]).

Figure 3.2. Reported change in financial situation during lockdown: Australia, France and Switzerland

Percentage of adults reporting change in financial situation

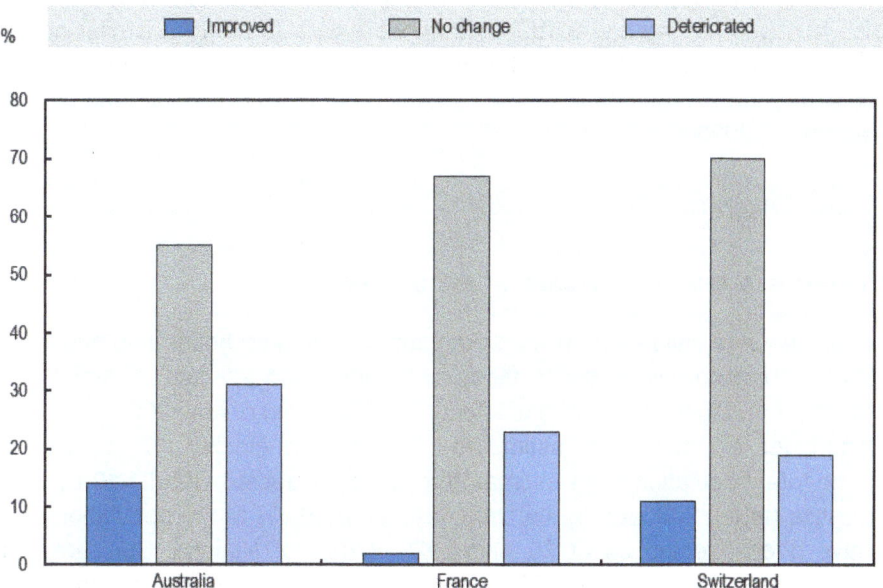

Notes: In France, 7% of the population reported that they did not know whether their financial situation had changed.
Population: Australia: persons 18 years and older; France: persons 15 years and older; Switzerland: persons 15-99 years of age.
Reference period: Australia: previous 4 weeks; France: period of confinement; Switzerland: period of lockdown.
Date of collection: Australia: 14-17 April 2020; France: May 2020; Switzerland: 12 May-20 June 2020.
Sources: Australia: (Australian Bureau of Statistics (ABS), 2020[9], Table 4.1); France: (Givord and Silhol, 2020[8], Complimentary Figure 1); Switzerland: (Refle et al., 2020[14]).

StatLink https://stat.link/opxmby

As can be seen, the majority of adults in each of these three countries experienced no change to their financial situation with the proportion experiencing a deterioration outweighing that experiencing an improvement.

A similar picture is observed in other countries. In Ireland, extremely small proportions of the adult population reported financial difficulties as a consequence of the COVID-19 pandemic in April 2020, with 3% of the population aged 15 years and over reporting that they are unable to pay bills, 5% deferring bills and 2% reporting rent or mortgage payment difficulties. The highest rates were reported by the 35-44 years age group for the deferment of bills, rent, and mortgage payment difficulties (Central Statistical Office (CSO), 2020[6]). Some 25% of the UK population aged 16-69 years reported that their household finances were being affected by COVID-19 in May 2020 (Office for National Statistics (ONS), 2020[15]).

Unsurprisingly, the incidence of financial difficulties was negatively related to income. Low income households in France were more likely to suffer a worsening of their financial situation due to lockdowns than high-income households (Albouy and Legleye, 2020[23]; Bajos et al., 2020[12]; Givord and Silhol, 2020[8]) and, in the United Kingdom, adults with low incomes were more likely to report a decline in income since the start of the Coronavirus pandemic than those with high incomes (Office for National Statistics (ONS), 2020[7]).

Parents in households with dependent children also appeared to be worse affected financially by lockdowns than other adults. In France, 33% of households with children reported a worsening of their financial situation compared to 18% of other households (Givord and Silhol, 2020[8]). The finances of parents in the United Kingdom were more affected during the initial weeks of lockdown (3 April to 10 May) than those of other adults. They were less likely to say they are able to save for the year ahead (20%) than other adults (43%). In terms of meeting unexpected expenses, 45% of parents reported being able to afford an unexpected but necessary expense of GBP 850 compared to 61% of adults without dependent children in the household. This was around one-third less than were able to afford a similar necessary expense before lockdown in 2018 (Office for National Statistics (ONS), 2020[7]). In Switzerland, over 30% of single parents indicated a deterioration of their financial situation, compared to 15% among those living only with their partner (Refle et al., 2020[14]).

The health situation in families

COVID-19 infections in the households of schoolchildren

The chances of a school age child either having the virus or living in a household in which someone was infected with COVID-19 were low. Even in those countries most affected, a small proportion of the population was infected during the first wave of infections. At the end of May 2020, 4.5% of the population aged 15 years and older in France were estimated to have been infected (Warszawski et al., 2020[24]). In Italy, 2.5% of the total population were estimated to have contracted COVID-19 by July 2020 (Istituto Nazionale di Statistica (Istat), 2020[25]). In the United Kingdom, 6.3% of the population aged 16 and over was found to have been infected as at 29 June 2020 (Office of National Statistics (ONS), 2020[26]). In all three countries, the national average hides considerable regional differences (e.g. with high rates in the Île-de-France in France, Lombardy in Italy and London in the United Kingdom).

Rates of infection and COVID-19-related deaths varied across different social and occupational groups. In particular, infection and death rates were higher among the population living in areas of high as opposed to low socio-economic deprivation in England and France and among certain ethnic groups, e.g. Blacks and Asians in the United Kingdom, first and second generation non-European immigrants in France and Blacks and Hispanics/Latinos in the United States [see for England, Public Health England (2020[27]); for France, Warszawski et al. (2020[24]); and for the United States, United States Center for Disease Control and Preventions (USDCP) (2021[28])]. Evidence from England and France indicates that workers in frontline healthcare occupations experienced particularly high infection rates (Warszawski et al., 2020[24]; Ward et al., 2021[29]). "Essential workers" in other sectors also experienced higher than average infection rates in the United Kingdom, but not in France. In addition, in both England and France, the incidence of infection was higher for persons living in households with 3 or more members (a category including most families with school age children) than those living in a household with 2 or less members (Warszawski et al., 2020[24]; Ward et al., 2021[29]).

Table 3.4. COVID-19 among household members and relatives, colleagues and friends: France and Switzerland

Status	France	Switzerland
Respondent infected	3%	1%
Household member infected	4%	<1%
Close relatives or friends infected	24%	9%
Work Colleague infected	n/a	8%
Member of wider circle of friends and acquaintances infected	n/a	26%
Person close to respondent died	3%	n/a
Population	Persons aged 18 and over	Persons aged 14 years and over
Date of data collection	7-10 May	May-June 2020

Sources: France: (Coconel, 2020[30]); Switzerland: (Refle et al., 2020[14], Table 3.1).

The probability of infection among household members' wider circle of family and friends was far greater than that of infection of surveyed persons or other household members (Table 3.4). For instance, in Switzerland, only 1% of respondents in the Swiss Household Panel COVID-19 study declared that they had contracted the virus by May/June 2020. Nine percent reported that a family member or close friend has been infected, whereas 26% reported that there was a COVID-19 case in their circle of friends and acquaintances (Refle et al., 2020[14]).

Mental health and well-being among adults

Mental and psychological health and well-being was a focus of many national level surveys of the impact of the Coronavirus pandemic on the adult population. Measures of psychological well-being such as anxiety, depression, and problems with sleep and life satisfaction have been collected on a regular basis since the start of the pandemic in a number of countries. While related, the exact concepts measured and the measures used differ between studies. Direct comparisons of levels are therefore difficult. However, trends can be compared.

The rapid spread of the COVID-19 virus, together with the lockdowns of March-June 2020, was associated with reductions in psychological well-being across the adult population. In countries in which data are available, broadly similar patterns are observed over the period of confinement/lockdown and the subsequent removal or reduction of restrictions on movement and social contacts. The levels of psychological well-being among adults as measured at the start of confinement were far below those measured pre-confinement but tended to improve with time as lockdowns continued and eased (though not for all problems or in all countries) (Table 3.5).

Data from France and the United States indicate that the levels of anxiety and depression were highest for adults in low status occupations, with low levels of education, low incomes and suffering financial hardship during lockdowns and after (Santé publique France, 2020[31]) and (United States Census Bureau, 2020[32], Health Tables 2a and 2b). It is not, however, possible to determine whether the psychological well-being of adults from disadvantaged social backgrounds was disproportionately affected by lockdowns compared to that of their advantaged peers.

Evidence from Canada, France and the United Kingdom suggests that the psychological health of parents of school age children may have been affected more by lockdowns than that of other adults. A study in Canada conducted in the second half of May 2020 (Gadermann et al., 2021[33]) found that a higher proportion of parents (44%) reported a deterioration in mental health since the onset of the COVID-19 pandemic than did their counterparts without children of less than 18 years at home (36%). In France, at the start of the period of confinement (23-25 March), 37% of parents with children aged 16 years or less reported high levels of anxiety compared to 22% of the rest of the population. The gap between the level of anxiety of parents of infants and school age children and other adults declined over the next months. However, it remained between 4 to 8 percentage points higher among parents with school age children than among other adults. In contrast, there was little difference in the incidence of depressive symptoms between parents with children aged 16 years and less and other adults (Figure 3.3). Finally, in the United Kingdom, the proportion of adults with at least one child under the age of 16 years displayed depressive symptoms during the pandemic increased by 15 percentage points (from 6% to 20%) compared to an increase of 10 percentage points among the adult population on as a whole (Office for National Statistics (ONS), 2020[34]).

Table 3.5. Psychological well-being: prior to, at the start of and following lockdowns in March-June 2020

Country	Measure	Pre-confinement % of population or average scale score (*)	During lockdown % of population or average scale score (*)	After lockdown % of population or average scale score (*)
Australia	Nervous	20	35	25
	Hopeless	9	11	8
	Restless or fidgety	24	42	25
	Everything was an effort	22	26	19
Canada	Life satisfaction (scale 0-10)	8.1*	n/a	6.7*
Finland	Stress	n/a	51	46
France	Life satisfaction	85	66	81
	Anxiety	14	27	15
	Depression[1]	n/a	20	11
	Depression[2]	11	14	n/a
	Sleep problems	49	61	62
Germany	Loneliness (scale 0-12)	3*	5.4*	n/a
	Depression or anxiety (scale 0-12)	1.9*	2.4*	n/a
	Life satisfaction (scale 0-10)	7.4*	7.4*	n/a
Ireland	High life satisfaction (scale 0-10)	8.1*	6.5*	7.0*
	Feeling downhearted or depressed (all/most of the time)	2.8	5.5	11.5
	Feeling Lonely (all/most of the time)	3.5	6.8	13.7
New Zealand	Depression or anxiety related symptoms	n/a	13	6
Switzerland	Life satisfaction (scale 0-10)	8*	n/a	8*
United Kingdom	Depression (moderate to severe symptoms)	10	19	19
	High anxiety	21	50	28
United States	Symptoms of anxiety disorder	8	31	31
	Symptoms of depressive disorder	7	24	36

* Average scale score.

Sources: Australia: (Australian Bureau of Statistics (ABS), 2020[35]); Canada: (Helliwell, Schellenberg and Fonberg, 2020[36]); Finland: (Statistics Finland, 2020[37]). Dates: 2-5 April 2020, 11-14 June 2020; France: (1) (Santé publique France, 2020[31]). Dates: Pre-confinement: January-July 2017, Confinement: 23-25 March 2020, 22-24 June 2020; (2) (Hazo and Costemalle, 2021[38]); Germany: (Entringer et al., 2020[39]). Dates: 2019 (2017 for loneliness), April 2020; Ireland: (Central Statistics Office (CSO), 2021[40]). Dates before: 2018, during lockdown: April 2020; after lockdown: August 2020 (life satisfaction), November 2020 (depression and loneliness); New Zealand: (Ministry of Health New Zealand, 2020[41]). Dates: week ending 5 April 2020, week ending 14 June 2020; Switzerland: (Refle et al., 2020[14]). Dates: 09.2019-03.2020 (95% of interviews completed before 17 December 2019), May/June 2020; United Kingdom: (Office for National Statistics (ONS), 2020[34]); United States: (National Center for Health Statistics (NCHS), n.d.[42]). Dates: Pre-confinement: January-June 2019, confinement: 23 April-5 May 2020, 18-23 June 2020.

Figure 3.3. Proportion of total population aged 16 years and over and of parents with children aged 16 years or less experiencing high anxiety

March to December 2020, France

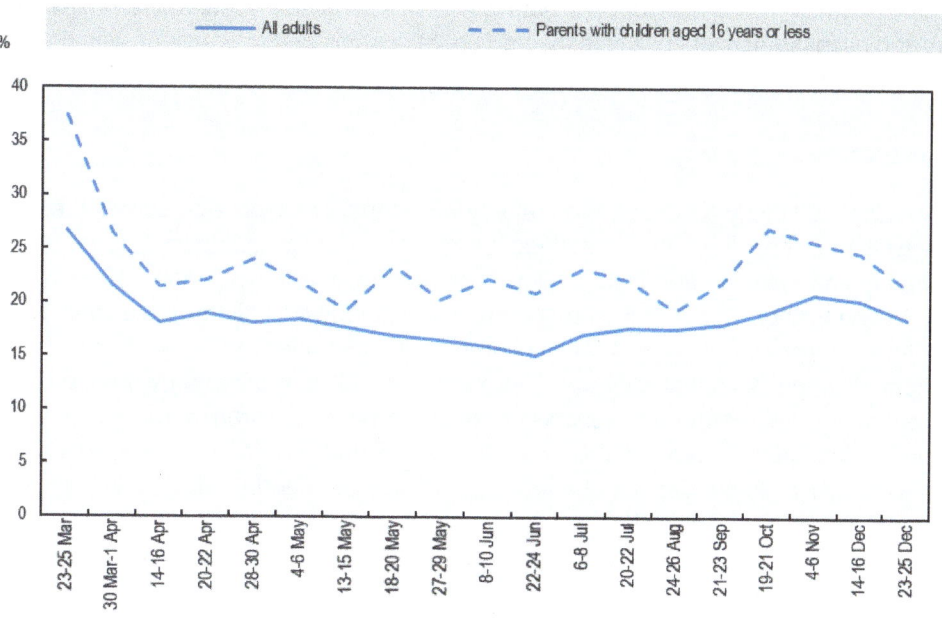

Source: (Santé publique France, 2020[31]).

StatLink https://stat.link/psz42u

Two other French studies provide a more nuanced insight into the relationship of mental health difficulties with parenthood during lockdown. In particular, the experience of single parents and parents living as a couple may have been very different. For example, adults living in a couple with children (24%) were less likely to have found confinement hard to deal with ("pénible") than single parents (29%) (Albouy and Legleye, 2020[23]). Similarly, parents living in a couple with children at home (9%) were much less likely than single parents (21%) to report symptoms of a depressive syndrome in May 2020 (Hazo and Costemalle, 2021[38]).

The burden of caring for children and supporting their education in circumstances in which they did not necessarily feel they had the time, resources or expertise to do so may have been one factor contributing to the greater levels of pyschological problems among parents than among other adults. As noted above, many parents did not feel well prepared or confident in their ability to assist their children with their education at home and a significant minority of parents found it difficult to balance work and childcare/homeschooling responsibilites during the period of school closures. There is evidence that their children and their children's education was a source of stress and worry for some, though far from all, parents during lockdowns. In second half of May 2020, among the possible stressors resulting from COVID-19 in the previous 2 weeks, 52% of Canadian parents cited worry about their children's education, 52% cited worry about how the mental health of their child(ren) was being affected and 37% reported being stressed about looking after children while continuing to work (Gadermann et al., 2021[33]). Among Swiss parents, 19% felt overwhelmed sometimes by having their child(ren) at home and 21% reported more tensions when everyone was at home (Refle et al., 2020[14]). Some 28% of the UK parents who had home-schooled their children in the previous week felt that home schooling was negatively affecting their own well-being (Office for National Statistics (ONS), 2020[10], Table 1).

Family relationships

Lockdowns and school closures had mixed consequences for parent/child relationships with both negative and positive effects reported. On balance, however, the impact seems to have been more positive than negative. The information available covers both general and global evaluations of the state of family relationships and assessments of specific aspects of relationships and interactions with children and other household/family members.

The general picture

In both France and the United Kingdom, the majority of parents of school age children reported that their relationships with their child(ren) had remained unchanged during lockdown (Figure 3.4). Among the parents reporting changes in their relationships, an improvement was more often reported than a deterioration. In one French study, 73% of respondents confined with children (less than 18 years of age) stated that their relationships with their children had remained the same compared with the pre-confinement situation, 16% that they had improved and 11% that they had worsened (Lambert et al., 2020[43]). In another French study of the parents of a cohort of children born in 2011 (i.e. who were 8 - 9 years old in May 2020), very similar results were found: 61% of parents indicated that their relationships with their children had not changed, 23% that they had improved and 16% that they were more tense than normal. This was also true for relationships between siblings (Thierry et al., 2021[44]). Likewise, in the United Kingdom, 70% of parents surveyed at the end of May reported that their relationships with their children (aged under 18 years) had remained "about the same", 26% that they were "better than before" with only 4% reporting that they were "worse than before" (Benzeval et al., 2020[45]). Another study of 5-16 year-olds in England (NHS Digital, 2020[46]) found no change in family functioning between 2017 and 2020 based on parents' reports.

Figure 3.4. Parents' relationship with children during confinement compared to before: France and United Kingdom

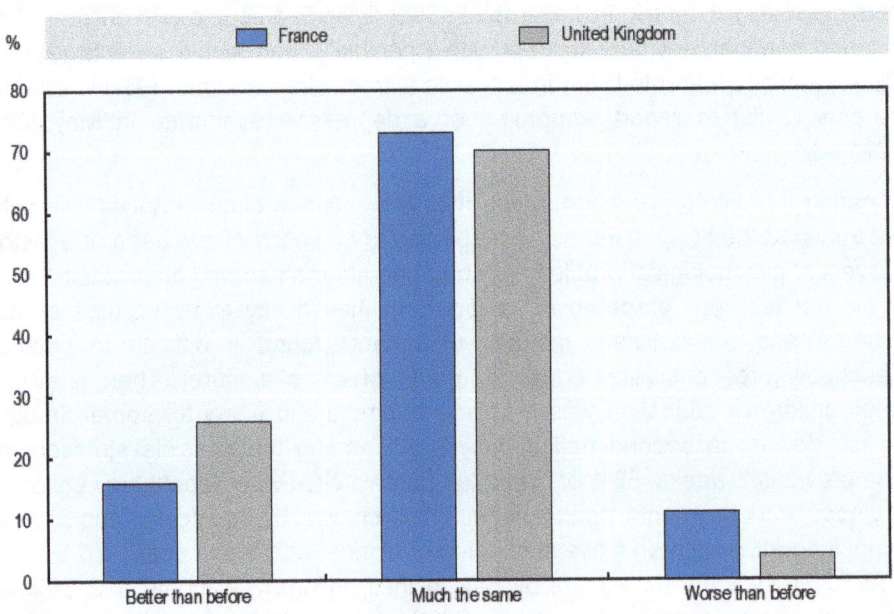

Sources: France: (Lambert et al., 2020[43]); United Kingdom: (Benzeval et al., 2020[45]).

StatLink https://stat.link/zubqlf

Positive global evaluations of family experience were expressed by adults in Ireland and Italy. Nearly half (46%) of Irish adults stated that they had experienced an increase in positive family time in April 2020 with the proportions being highest (54%) among 35-44 and 45-54 year-olds, the age groups most likely to have dependent children (Central Statistical Office (CSO), 2020[6]). When asked to define the family climate prevailing during the first period of lockdown, three out of four Italians used positive descriptors. Less than 15% chose neutral descriptors and only 8% used terms with negative connotations (Istituto Nazionale di Statistica (Istat), 2020[47], Figure 1).

Relationships in more detail

Parents and children identified a range of negative and positive aspects of family relationships and interpersonal interactions during lockdowns. For the most part, the negative aspects were reported as being experienced by smaller proportions of respondents than the positive aspects.

Many studies report that the period of lockdowns was accompanied by an increase in family tensions and strains on relationships, generally in a minority of cases. Canadian parents reported more negative interactions with their children due to the COVID-19 pandemic, including more conflicts (22%), yelling/shouting (17%), disciplining (16%) and using harsh words (11%) (Gadermann et al., 2021[33]). Dutch 8-18 year-olds reported a worse atmosphere at home during the COVID-19 lockdown than before COVID-19 (Luijten et al., 2021[48]). Some 28% of the parents of French secondary school students agreed that living in confinement had created family conflicts (Direction de l'évaluation de la prospective et de la performance (DEPP), 2020[49], Figure 5-6) and one out of five French adults (19%) had experienced a particularly difficult moment due to a conflict with another person with whom he/she had been confined either once (9%) or several times (10%) (Lambert et al., 2020[43]). In Germany, 28% of children and adolescents reported that arguments had increased in the family and 30% of parents stated that disputes escalated more often (Ravens-Sieberer et al., 2021[50]). This matches results from another survey where 28% of parents with school age children reported to have argued more with their child(ren) during school closures (Wößmann et al., 2020[51]). In Israel, 23% of adults who did not live alone reported a moderate to great degree of tension among members of their household in the wake of the pandemic, with the level rising to 27% among members of households with four or more persons (those most likely to include school age children) (Central Bureau of Statistics, 2020[52]). Among Swiss parents, 21% agreed that there were "more tensions when everyone was at home" and 19% agreed that that they were sometimes overwhelmed by having the children at home (Refle et al., 2020[14]). Finally, 36% of adults in the United Kingdom who home schooled children agreed that home schooling was putting a strain on their relationships with others in the household (Office for National Statistics (ONS), 2020[10], Table 1).

While spending more time together than in normal circumstances may have increased tensions among family members in some families, it also had its positive side. Canadian parents reported that they experienced increased positive interactions with their children during lockdowns, including having more quality time (65%), feeling closeness (50%), showing love or affection to their children (45%) and observing increased resilience and perseverance in their children (38%) (Gadermann et al., 2021[33]). Nearly three-quarters (74%) of the parents of secondary students in France felt that living in confinement had allowed them to have new relationships with their children and 69% that it had allowed them to undertake different activities as a family (Direction de l'évaluation de la prospective et de la performance (DEPP), 2020[49], Figure 5-6). As previously noted, French parents spent more time than usual with their children undertaking educational activities in the period of confinement. This was also true for leisure activities though to a much less marked degree. Some 40% of the parents of secondary students stated that they spent more time than normal in leisure activities with their children with 28% spending less and 25% spending as much time as usual (Direction de l'évaluation de la prospective et de la performance (DEPP), 2020[49]). A high proportion of Swiss parents (73%) also agreed that the period of school closures constituted an opportunity to spend more time with their child(ren) (Refle et al., 2020[14]).

The evidence regarding the associations between socio-economic background and family relationships is relatively limited and, where it exists, contradictory. In France, one study (Lambert et al., 2020[43]) found that the parent/child relationships improved more for parents in low status than high status occupations and that parents who were teleworking were more likely than those working outside the home to report a worsening in their relationships with children. Another (Thierry et al., 2021[44]) found the reverse: relationships more often improved among households headed by persons in professional or managerial occupations and for parents who were teleworking, independent of their occupational status. In the United Kingdom, no relationship was observed between family income and change in parent/child relationships due to lockdowns. However, parents spending more time with their children tended to be more likely to report that their relationships had improved (31% of parents working at home compared to 24% of those who were not) (Benzeval et al., 2020[45]).

Use of leisure time

Several studies offer an insight into how children spent their leisure time during lockdown. Given that students spent on average less time on educational activities compared to the pre-pandemic period (and did not spent time travelling to school), they had more "free" time at their disposal. However, the types of activity that could be undertaken during this free time was severely constrained by restrictions on movement, social contact and the time that could be spent outside one's place of residence. In particular, activities such as organised sports were and spending time in the physical presence of friends were impossible. How did child-age children use this time? What was the balance between physical activities such as sport or playing outside and sedentary behaviours such as watching television or using their smartphones?

Surveys from France, Germany and Switzerland provide information on the changes in the time spent on physical activity and screen-based activities during lockdown compared to life pre-lockdown. Both the time spent on screen-based activities and time spent on physical activities appears to have increased with the increase being greatest for screen-based activities. According to their parents, French secondary school students were more likely to have increased the amount of time spent on screen-based activities such as watching series and films (71%), playing video games (54%) and using the Internet for work (81%) or leisure (60%) than on either reading (23%) or physical activity (23%). Girls were more likely than boys to increase the time spent on reading and physical activity. Boys were far more likely than girls to have increased the amount of time spent playing video games. In Germany, the time spent by school children on sports activity declined by on average 10.8 minutes per day due to the closure of organised sports (Schmidt et al., 2020[53]). Nevertheless, this decline was more than offset by an increase in other physical activities such as playing outside, walking, cycling, housework and gardening. Recreational screen time increased during lockdown compared to the pre-lockdown period. Time spent gaming and watching TV increased by 21 minutes per day, while recreational Internet usage increased by 18 minutes (Schmidt et al., 2020[53]). In Switzerland, some aspects of physical activity increased during lockdown. For example, the number of days during which adolescents practiced a physical activity that made them slightly breathless for at least half an hour increased from less than three days to almost four days during lockdown (Refle et al., 2020[14]).

Summary

Lockdowns affected the home environment of school children in many ways. Restrictions on movement outside the home and on social contact limited in-person social interaction essentially to members of the household. A large proportion of parents were at home with their children due to loss of employment, the temporary closure of their workplaces or because they were required to work at home all or some of the time. Schoolchildren were, on average, very unlikely to live in a household in which a household member had been infected by the virus (acknowledging the wide variation in infection rates across regions within countries), but were much more likely to know someone who had caught the virus among their wider social and family network. The psychological well-being of adults declined dramatically with the start of lockdowns but progressively improved as lockdowns continued and restrictions were reduced and eventually, removed, with the parents of school age children and infants being affected more severely than the adult population as a whole. Overall, income support and job retention schemes appear to have buffered the negative effects of the administrative closure of businesses and workplaces on incomes. However, parents with dependent children appear to have been worse affected than other adults.

School closures meant that parents had to take on responsibilities for childcare and the supervision of schooling that were normally undertaken by schools and/or other persons (e.g. family members, paid carers) or organisations. The impact of this on the working hours and working arrangements of parents was mitigated by the fact that many parents were, themselves, at home due to lockdowns. Nevertheless, a significant minority of parents had to stop working or reduce working hours to look after young children and to provide support for their education. Women were more likely to do this than men. Overall, it appears that most parents found ways of managing the situation and did not find balancing work and family life and/or working from home to be a source of difficulty or stress.

Lockdowns and school closures do not appear to have had a significant negative or positive impact on family life and parent/child relationships. On the one hand, tensions between family members may have increased but, on the other, the opportunities to spend more time with children and to undertake new activities also increased.

References

Albouy, V. and S. Legleye (2020), "Conditions de vie pendant le confinement : des écarts selon le niveau de vie et la catégorie socioprofessionnelle", *Insee Focus n°197*, https://www.insee.fr/fr/statistiques/4513259#documentation. [23]

Amuedo-Dorantes, C., M. Marcén, M. Morales and A. Sevilla (2020), *COVID-19 School Closures and Parental Labor Supply in the United States*, IZA DP No.13827, http://ftp.iza.org/dp13827.pdf. [20]

Australian Bureau of Statistics (ABS) (2020), *Coronavirus (COVID-19) impacts on jobs, lifestyle, stressors, wellbeing, moving, health precautions and use of health services. Reference period: 24-29 June 2020, Australia*, https://www.abs.gov.au/statistics/people/people-and-communities/household-impacts-covid-19-survey/24-29-june-2020. [35]

Australian Bureau of Statistics (ABS) (2020), *Household Impacts of COVID-19 Survey, Coronavirus (COVID-19) impacts on psychological distress, contact with family and friends, financial stress and stimulus payments received. Reference period: 14-17 April 2020, Australia*, https://www.abs.gov.au/statistics/people/people-and-communities/household-impacts-covid-19-survey/14-17-apr-2020#data-download. [9]

Australian Bureau of Statistics (ABS) (2020), *Household Impacts of COVID-19 Survey, Coronavirus impacts on job situation, health services, health precautions, social distancing, household stressors, support network, lifestyle changes. Reference period: 29 April-4 May 2020, Australia*, https://www.abs.gov.au/statistics/people/people-and-communities/household-impacts-covid-19-survey/29-apr-4-may-2020. [11]

Australian Bureau of Statistics (ABS) (2020), *Household Impacts of COVID-19 Survey, Coronavirus impacts on job status, JobKeeper, superannuation, loan repayments, living arrangements, childcare, schooling and care provided. Reference period: 12-15 May 2020, Australia*, https://www.abs.gov.au/statistics/people/people-and-communities/household-impacts-covid-19-survey/12-15-may-2020. [4]

Australian Bureau of Statistics (ABS) (2019), *Characteristics of Employment, Australia Weekly earnings of employees classified by full-time/part-time workers, employment characteristics and fixed-term/independent contracts. Reference period: August 2019, Australia*, https://www.abs.gov.au/statistics/labour/earnings-and-work-hours/characteristics-employment-australia/latest-release. [16]

Bajos, N., J. Warszawski, A. Pailhé, E. Counil, F. Jusot, A. Spire, C. Martin, L. Meyer, A. Sireyjol, J-E. Franck, N. Lydié (2020), "Les inégalités sociales au temps du Covid-19", *Questions de santé publique n°40, Institut pour la Recherche en Santé Publique (IReSP)*, https://www.iresp.net/wp-content/uploads/2020/10/IReSP_QSP40.web_.pdf. [12]

Benzeval, M., J. Burton, TF. Crossley, P. Fisher, A. Jäckle, B. Perelli-Harris and S. Walzenbach (2020), "Understanding Society COVID-19 Survey May Briefing Note: Family relationships", *Understanding Society Working Paper No. 13/2020*, Institute for Social and Economic Research (ISER), University of Essex, https://www.understandingsociety.ac.uk/sites/default/files/downloads/general/ukhls_briefingnote_covid_family_final.pdf. [45]

Bureau of Labor Statistics (BLS) (2020), *Supplemental data measuring the effects of the coronavirus (COVID-19) pandemic on the labor market, Effects of the coronavirus COVID-19 pandemic (CPS)*, https://www.bls.gov/cps/effects-of-the-coronavirus-covid-19-pandemic.htm#data,%20May%20data%20tables. [3]

Central Bureau of Statistics (2020), *Civilian Resilience in Israel and the COVID-19 Pandemic: Analysis of a CBS Survey*, INSS Insight No. 1318, https://www.inss.org.il/publication/coronavirus-survey/. [52]

Central Statistical Office (CSO) (2020), *Employment and Life Effects of COVID-19 April 2020. CSO statistical release, 13 May 2020, Ireland*, https://www.cso.ie/en/releasesandpublications/er/elec19/employmentandlifeeffectsofcovid-19/. [6]

Central Statistics Office (CSO) (2021), *Social Impact of COVID-19 Survey February 2021: Well-being*, https://www.cso.ie/en/releasesandpublications/ep/p-sic19wbg/socialimpactofcovid-19surveyfebruary2021well-being/resultsandanalysis/. [40]

Coconel (2020), *Note de synthèse n°11. Opinions sur le (dé)confinement, moments difficiles, sorties et santé*, Coconel (COronavirus et CONfinement, enquête longitudinale), vague 7, France, http://www.orspaca.org/sites/default/files/coconel-note-de-synthese-11-opinions-deconfinement-sorties-sante.pdf. [30]

Direction de l'évaluation, de la prospective et de la performance (DEPP) (2020), *Confinement : un investissement scolaire important des élèves du second degré, essentiellement différencié selon leur niveau scolaire, Note d'information n° 20.42*, Ministère de l'Éducation nationale, de la Jeunesse et des Sports, https://www.education.gouv.fr/confinement-un-investissement-scolaire-important-des-eleves-du-second-degre-essentiellement-307441. [54]

Direction de l'évaluation de la prospective et de la performance (DEPP) (2020), *Continuité pédagogique - période de mars à mai 2020 - enquêtes de la DEPP auprès des familles et des personnels de l'Éducation nationale – premiers résultats*, Document de travail n°2020-E03, Ministère de l'Education nationale, de la Jeunesse et des Sports, https://www.education.gouv.fr/continuite-pedagogique-periode-de-mars-mai-2020-enquetes-de-la-depp-aupres-des-familles-et-des-305262. [49]

Entringer, T., H. Kröger, J. Schupp, S. Kühne, S. Liebig, J. Goebel, M.M. Grabka, D. Graeber, M. Kroh, C. Schröder, J. Seebauer and S. Zinn (2020), *Psychische Krise durch Covid-19? Sorgen sinken, Einsamkeit steigt, Lebenszufriedenheit bleibt stabil*, https://www.diw.de/documents/publikationen/73/diw_01.c.791307.de/diw_sp1087.pdf. [39]

Felstead, A. and D. Reuschke (2020), *Homeworking in the UK: Before and during the 2020 lockdown*, WISERD Report, Wales Institute of Social and Economic Research, Cardiff, https://wiserd.ac.uk/sites/default/files/documents/Homeworking%20in%20the%20UK_Report_Final_3.pdf. [17]

Foucault, M. and V. Galasso (2020), *Working After Covid-19: Cross-Country Evidence from Real-Time Survey Data*, Note on Attitudes towards COVID-19 - A comparative study, Sciences Po CEVIPOF, note 9, https://www.sciencespo.fr/cevipof/attitudesoncovid19/wp-content/uploads/2020/05/Note9_FOUCAULT_GALASSO_ENG.pdf. [55]

Gadermann, A., K. Thomson, C. Richardson, M. Gagné, C. McAuliffe, S. Hirani and E. Jenkins (2021), "Examining the impacts of the COVID-19 pandemic on family mental health in Canada: findings from a national cross-sectional study", *BMJ Open*, Vol. 11/1, p. e042871, http://dx.doi.org/10.1136/bmjopen-2020-042871. [33]

Givord, P. and J. Silhol (2020), "Confinement : des conséquences économiques inégales selon les ménages", *Insee Première, No. 1822*, https://www.insee.fr/fr/statistiques/4801313#documentation. [8]

Hazo, J. and V. Costemalle (2021), "Confinement du printemps 2020 : une hausse des syndromes dépressifs, surtout chez les 15-24 ans. Résultats issus de la 1e vague de l'enquête EpiCov et comparaison avec les enquêtes de santé européennes (EHIS) de 2014 et 2019", *Études et résultats, n°1185, mars 2021*, https://drees.solidarites-sante.gouv.fr/publications/etudes-et-resultats/confinement-du-printemps-2020-une-hausse-des-syndromes-depressifs. [38]

Heggeness, M. and J. Fields (2020), *Working Moms Bear Brunt of Home Schooling While Working During COVID-19*, US Census Bureau, August 18, 2020, https://www.census.gov/library/stories/2020/08/parents-juggle-work-and-child-care-during-pandemic.html. [19]

Helliwell, J., G. Schellenberg and J. Fonberg (2020), *Satisfaction à l'égard de la vie au Canada avant et pendant la pandémie de COVID-19*, Direction des études analytiques : documents de recherche, Statistiques Canada, Ottawa, https://www150.statcan.gc.ca/n1/pub/45-28-0001/2020001/article/00093-fra.htm. [36]

Istituto Nazionale di Statistica (Istat) (2020), *Primi Risultati dell'indagine di Sieroprevalenza sul SARS-CoV-2*, https://www.istat.it/it/files/2020/08/ReportPrimiRisultatiIndagineSiero.pdf. [25]

Istituto Nazionale di Statistica (Istat) (2020), *Reazione dei Cittadini al Lockdown: 5 Aprile–21 Aprile 2020*, https://www.istat.it/it/files/2020/05/Reazione_cittadini_lockdown.pdf. [47]

Jauneau, Y. and J. Vidalenc (2020), "Durée travaillée et travail à domicile pendant le confinement : des différences marquées selon les professions", *Insee Focus No 207 - octobre*, https://www.insee.fr/fr/statistiques/4801229#consulter. [5]

Jones, J. (2020), *Social Factors Most Challenging in COVID-19 Distance Learning, Gallup Panel, 11-24 May 2020*, https://news.gallup.com/poll/312566/social-factors-challenging-covid-distance-learning.aspx. [21]

Lambert, A., J. Cayouette-Remblière, E. Guéraut, C. Bonvalet, V. Girard, G. Le Roux, L. Langlois (2020), *Logement, travail, voisinage et conditions de vie : ce que le confinement a changé pour les Français - Note de synthèse n°10, Vague 6*, Coconel (COronavirus et CONfinement, enquête longitudinale) and Institut national d'études démographiques (INED), http://www.orspaca.org/sites/default/files/coconel-note-10-logement-travail-voisinage-conditions-de-vie_ined.pdf. [43]

Leskinen, T. (2020), *Regularly working at home has doubled*, Statistics Finland, Blog post 22/12/2020, https://www.stat.fi/tietotrendit/blogit/2020/saannollisesti-kotona-tyoskenteleminen-on-kaksinkertaistunut/. [13]

Luijten, M., M. van Muilekom, L. Teela, T. Polderman, C. Terwee, J. Zijlmans, L. Klaufus, A. Popma, K. Oostrom, H. van Oers and L. Haverman (2021), "The impact of lockdown during the COVID-19 pandemic on mental and social health of children and adolescents", *Quality of Life Research*, http://dx.doi.org/10.1007/s11136-021-02861-x. [48]

Ministry of Health New Zealand (2020), *COVID-19 Health and Wellbeing Survey: Week 23 results*, https://www.health.govt.nz/our-work/diseases-and-conditions/covid-19-novel-coronavirus/covid-19-resources-and-tools/covid-19-health-and-wellbeing-survey. [41]

National Center for Health Statistics (NCHS) (n.d.), *Anxiety and Depression: Household Pulse Survey*, https://www.cdc.gov/nchs/covid19/pulse/mental-health.htm. [42]

NHS Digital (2020), *Mental Health of Children and Young People in England, 2020: Wave 1 follow up to the 2017 survey*, https://digital.nhs.uk/data-and-information/publications/statistical/mental-health-of-children-and-young-people-in-england/2020-wave-1-follow-up/data-sets. [46]

OECD (2021), *OECD Employment Outlook 2021: Navigating the COVID-19 Crisis and Recovery*, OECD Publishing, Paris, https://dx.doi.org/10.1787/5a700c4b-en. [1]

OECD.Stat (2020), *Short-Term Labour Market Statistics: Monthly Unemployment Rates, OECD Statistics*, http://dotstat.oecd.org/Index.aspx?QueryId=36324. [2]

Office for National Statistics (ONS) (2020), *Coronavirus and depression in adults, Great Britain: June 2020*, https://www.ons.gov.uk/peoplepopulationandcommunity/wellbeing/articles/coronavirusanddepressioninadultsgreatbritain/june2020. [34]

Office for National Statistics (ONS) (2020), *Coronavirus and homeschooling in Great Britain: April to June 2020. Analysis of homeschooling in Great Britain during the coronavirus (COVID-19) pandemic from the Opinions and Lifestyle Survey*, https://www.ons.gov.uk/peoplepopulationandcommunity/educationandchildcare/articles/coronavirusandhomeschoolingingreatbritain/apriltojune2020. [10]

Office for National Statistics (ONS) (2020), *Coronavirus and the social impacts on Great Britain: 22 May 2020*, https://www.ons.gov.uk/peoplepopulationandcommunity/healthandsocialcare/healthandwellbeing/bulletins/coronavirusandthesocialimpactsongreatbritain/22may2020. [15]

Office for National Statistics (ONS) (2020), *Personal and economic well-being in Great Britain: June 2020*, https://www.ons.gov.uk/peoplepopulationandcommunity/wellbeing/bulletins/personalandeconomicwellbeingintheuk/june2020. [7]

Office of National Statistics (ONS) (2020), *Coronavirus (COVID-19) Infection Survey pilot: England, 17 July 2020*, https://www.ons.gov.uk/peoplepopulationandcommunity/healthandsocialcare/conditionsanddiseases/bulletins/coronaviruscovid19infectionsurveypilot/england17july2020. [26]

Public Health England (2020), *Disparities in the risk and outcomes of COVID-19*, Public Health England, London, https://assets.publishing.service.gov.uk/government/uploads/system/uploads/attachment_data/file/908434/Disparities_in_the_risk_and_outcomes_of_COVID_August_2020_update.pdf. [27]

Ravens-Sieberer, U., A. Kaman, M. Erhart, J. Devine, R. Schlack and C. Otto (2021), "Impact of the COVID-19 pandemic on quality of life and mental health in children and adolescents in Germany", *European Child & Adolescent Psychiatry*, http://dx.doi.org/10.1007/s00787-021-01726-5. [50]

Refle, J., M. Voorpostel, F. Lebert, U. Kuhn, H.S. Klaas, V.-A. Ryser, N. Dasoki, G.-A. Monsch, E. Antal and R. Tillmann (2020), "First results of the Swiss Household Panel – Covid-19 Study", *FORS Working Paper Series*, No. 2020-1, FORS, Lausanne, https://forscenter.ch/working-papers/first-results-of-the-swiss-household-panel-covid-19-study/. [14]

Santé publique France (2020), *Enquête CoviPrev, une enquête pour suivre l'évolution des comportements et de la santé mentale pendant l'épidémie de COVID-19*, https://www.santepubliquefrance.fr/etudes-et-enquetes/covid-19-une-enquete-pour-suivre-l-evolution-des-comportements-et-de-la-sante-mentale-pendant-l-epidemie. [31]

Schmidt, S., B. Anedda, A. Burchartz, A. Eichsteller, S. Kolb, C. Nigg, C. Niessner, D. Oriwol, A. Worth and A. Woll (2020), "Physical activity and screen time of children and adolescents before and during the COVID-19 lockdown in Germany: a natural experiment", *Scientific Reports*, Vol. 10/1, http://dx.doi.org/10.1038/s41598-020-78438-4. [53]

Statistics Finland (2020), *Citizen's Pulse Survey*, https://www.stat.fi/tup/htpalvelut/tutkimukset/kansalaispulssi.html. [37]

Thierry, X., B. Geay, A. Pailhé, N. Berthomier, J. Camus, N. Cauchi-Duval, J-L. Lanoë, S. Octobre, J. Pagis, L. Panico, T. Siméon, A. Solaz et l'équipe SAPRIS (2021), *Les enfants à l'épreuve du premier confinement*, Institut national d'études démographiques (Ined), https://www.ined.fr/fichier/s_rubrique/31037/585.enfants.confinement.population.societes.janvier.2021.fr.pdf. [44]

United States Census Bureau (2020), *Household Pulse Survey: Measuring Social and Economic Impacts during the Coronavirus Pandemic*, https://www.census.gov/programs-surveys/household-pulse-survey.html. [32]

United States Center for Disease Control and Preventions (USDCP) (2021), *Risk for COVID-19 Infection, Hospitalization, and Death By Race/Ethnicity*, https://www.cdc.gov/coronavirus/2019-ncov/covid-data/investigations-discovery/hospitalization-death-by-race-ethnicity.html. [28]

University of Southern California (USC) (2020), *Understanding Coronavirus in America, Methodology and Topline Results UAS 242*, Wave 4, April 29-May 26, 2020, University of Southern California, Dornsife Center for Economic and Social Research, https://uasdata.usc.edu/index.php. [22]

Viner, R., S. Russell, H. Croker, J. Packer, J. Ward, C. Stansfield, O. Mytton, C. Bonell, R. Booy, (2020), "School closure and management practices during coronavirus outbreaks including COVID-19: a rapid systematic review", *The Lancet Child & Adolescent Health*, Vol. 4/5, pp. 397-404, http://dx.doi.org/10.1016/s2352-4642(20)30095-x. [18]

Ward, H., C. Atchison, M. Whitaker, K. Ainslie, J. Elliott, L. Okell, R. Redd, D. Ashby, C. Donnelly, W. Barclay, A. Darzi, G. Cooke, S. Riley and P. Elliott (2021), "SARS-CoV-2 antibody prevalence in England following the first peak of the pandemic", *Nature Communications*, Vol. 12/1, http://dx.doi.org/10.1038/s41467-021-21237-w. [29]

Warszawski, J., N. Bajos, L. Meyer, X. de Lamballerie, R. Seng, A-L. Beaumont, R. Slama, M. Hisbergues, D. Rahib, N. Lydié, B. Legendre, M. Barlet, S. Rey, P. Raynaud, A. Leduc, V. Costemalle, F. Beck, S. Legleye, L. Castell, P. Givord, C. Favre-Martinoz, N. Paliod, J. Silhol and P. Sillard (2020), "En mai 2020, 4,5 % de la population vivant en France métropolitaine a développé des anticorps contre le SARS-CoV-2. Premiers résultats de l'enquête nationale EpiCov", *Études et Résultats n° 1167, octobre 2020, Drees*, https://drees.solidarites-sante.gouv.fr/sites/default/files/2020-10/er1167.pdf. [24]

Wößmann, L., V. Freundl, E. Grewenig, P. Lergetporer, K. Werner and L. Zierow (2020), "Bildung in der Coronakrise: Wie haben die Schulkinder die Zeit der Schulschließungen verbracht, und welche Bildungsmaßnahmen befürworten die Deutschen?", *ifo Schnelldienst*, Vol. 73/9, pp. 25-39, https://www.ifo.de/publikationen/2020/aufsatz-zeitschrift/bildung-der-coronakrise-wie-haben-die-schulkinder-die-zeit. [51]

Notes

[1] In 2019, most of the employed persons who worked zero hours in France were taking annual leave or sick leave.

[2] See also (Foucault and Galasso, 2020[55], Table 3). In a survey conducted in 12 countries, between 29% and 60% of adults usually employed in January 2020 were working at home in mid-April or end-April/early-May 2020.

[3] The source is different to that used for the UK data in Table 3.2.

[4] (Foucault and Galasso, 2020[55]).

[5] UK figures for May 2020.

[6] The proportion of mothers of secondary school students in France who reported that they had increased the frequency of educational activities with their children during the March-June lockdown compared to normal times (62%) was more than double that of fathers (28%) (Direction de l'évaluation, de la prospective et de la performance (DEPP), 2020[54], Figures 7 and 8).

[7] The data comes from the Household Pulse Survey.

[8] This represents 19.8% of the 67.3% of parents in employment who had at least one dependent child aged 5 to 18 years living in the household for whom the Coronavirus was affecting their work who stated that they were finding working from home difficult.

4 School children's psychological well-being and academic progress

The two previous chapters have examined the experience of schooling (during school closures in March to June 2020) and characteristics of the home situation of school age children. In this chapter, the available evidence regarding children's psychological well-being and academic progress during this period is examined. How well did school-age children cope with the period of lockdown and school closures? Was the academic progress of school children slowed during this period and, if so, to what extent?

Introduction

The two previous chapters have examined the experience of schooling (during school closures in March to June 2020) and characteristics of the home situation of school age children. In this chapter, the available evidence regarding children's psychological well-being and academic progress during this period is examined. How well did school-age children cope with the period of lockdown and school closures? Was the academic progress of school children slowed during this period and, if so, to what extent? The academic progress of children will be examined from two perspectives: the perceptions of parents and to a lesser extent teachers and students themselves, and the more "objective" perspectives of standardised tests when available.

The psychological well-being of children

Lockdowns and the associated closure of schools represented a dramatic disruption to the lives of school age children to which they had to adapt more or less overnight. How did school age children cope with the consequences for their lives of lockdowns, school closures and the presence of the COVID-19 virus? Relatively few representative studies on the mental health of children during lockdowns have been published.[1] The available information is sketchy and approaches the question from a range of different perspectives.

The concerns and feelings of children

Several studies provide an insight into the concerns and feelings of children during the period of lockdown. These include studies using self-reports of children and the reports of parents/guardians regarding their children (and, sometimes, both).

From the perspective of parents

Parents in England reported that their children (aged 5-16 years) were worried about missing school (40%) and that friends might catch COVID (37%) but were less worried about catching COVID themselves (22%) or infecting others (16%) (NHS Digital, 2020[1], Table 3.2). Just over half (52%) of the parents of secondary school students in France reported that their children were worried about the future (Direction de l'évaluation de la prospective et de la performance (DEPP), 2020[2]). Only a small proportion (13%) of parents of children born in 2011 in France (i.e. aged 8-9 years at the date of the survey) reported that their child experienced social-emotional difficulties such as isolation, anxiety, difficulties in concentrating and impulsiveness during the period of confinement (Thierry et al., 2021[3]). In the United States, the experience of lockdown by children did not seem to be overly negative, at least early on in the period. Nearly 90% parents reported that their children exerienced enjoyment (89%) and happiness (88%) for "a lot of the day" on the day before they were interviewed in March 2020 and the proportions of parents reporting that their children experienced "negative" emotions such as "worry", "stress", "anger", "sadness" and "loneliness" were in the range of 20%-26%. The only exception was "boredom" which was reported as being experienced by 65% of children (Jones, 2020[4]).

From the perspective of children

School age children reported a generally negative view of the impact of lockdowns on their life, although positive aspects were also noted. A majority of French school children surveyed at the start of the 2021 school year (September 2020) regarding the experience of confinement over April-June 2020 reported that the period of confinement had been too long (63% of children in grades K-1, 70% in year 5 and 54% in year 9) and that they had been affected by the absence of contact with their friends (75% of children in grades K-1, 82% in year 5 and 80% in year 9). Between 25% and 39% (depending on grade) had experienced a fear of Coronavirus and between 38-51% had experienced boredom. At the same time, a majority appreciated the ease of studying at home (57-61%) and between 36-56% expressed satisfaction at being able to remain at home all the time (Direction de l'évaluation, de la prospective et de la performance (DEPP), 2021[5], Tables 1-3).

In the Netherlands, almost all (90%) children (aged 8-18 years) reported that the COVID-19 lockdown had a negative impact on their daily life. The issues most often mentioned were: 1) missing contact with friends, 2) not being allowed to go to school, 3) missing freedom, 4) not being allowed to participate in sports, 5) missing joyful activities (e.g., birthdays, holidays, parties, shopping), 6) difficulties with homeschooling 7) missing extended family, and 8) boredom (Luijten et al., 2021[6], Table 5). Broadly similar results were found in Germany (Ravens-Sieberer et al., 2021[7]). Nearly two-thirds (71%) of German children (aged 11-17 years) stated that they felt burdened by the COVID-19 pandemic. Four out of five (83%) reported fewer social contacts during the pandemic, 64% found schooling and learning to be more difficult than before the pandemic and 39% reported that their relationships with their friends had been impaired. Children and adolescents also reported depressive symptoms: 62% had trouble concentrating, 58% had little interest or joy in activities, and 34% felt sad.

In contrast, a study in England found a more mixed appreciation of the period of lockdown with 43% of 11-16 year-olds reporting that it had made their life worse, 30% reporting that it had made no change and the remaining 27% reporting that it had made their life better (NHS Digital, 2020, p. 45[8]). Some 55% of children reported that they were hardly ever or never lonely with only 5% stating that they were often or always lonely during lockdown (NHS Digital, 2020[1], Table 3.6).

Change in psychological well-being

In addition to understanding how children felt about and reacted to the situation of lockdown and school closures, a key question for evaluating the impact of lockdowns/school closures on the pyschological health and well-being of children is whether it was associated with change in their pyschological state.

From the perspective of parents

In the studies reviewed, a sizable minority of parents reported a worsening of their child(ren)'s psychological welbeing during lockdown. In a Canadian study, 25% of parents indicated that their children's mental health had worsened since the onset of the COVID-19 pandemic with the majority of parents (60%) reporting their children's mental health had stayed the same (Gadermann et al., 2021[9]). Parents in Germany reported that their children (aged 7-17 years) suffered from more mental health problems during than prior to the pandemic. The prevalence of noticeable mental health problems was 10% before the pandemic and increased to 18% during the pandemic. This increase was greatest among 7-10 year-olds (from 7 to 27%). At the same time, declines in the incidence of emotional symptoms, conduct problems, hyperactivity and peer problems were reported (Ravens-Sieberer et al., 2021[7]). In a survey conducted in Israel in the first week of April 2020, 28% of parents stated that their children's emotional state had deteriorated as a result of lockdown (Central Bureau of Statistics, 2020[10]) and, in the United Kingdom, 43% of parents home schooling their children agreed that remote schooling was negatively affecting their children's well-being (Office for National Statistics (ONS), 2020[11], Table 1).

From the perspective of children

Studies based on the reports of children themselves provide contrasting results. A national mental health cohort study in England (Figure 4.1) found that the proportion of 5-16 year-olds who were unlikely to have a mental disorder had remained unchanged between 2017 and July 2020 at around 74-75% (NHS Digital, 2020[1], Table 1.1). The main change between 2017 and 2020 was that the estimated proportion of children with a "probable" disorder increased by 5 percentage points and the proportion with a "possible" disorder declined by the same margin. In Germany, children and adolescents (11-17 years of age) were found to have lower health related quality of life (HRQoL)[2] during than prior to the pandemic. Before the pandemic, 15% of children and adolescents reported low HRQoL, increasing to 40% during lockdown, with the increase being greater for younger than older children (Ravens-Sieberer et al., 2021[7]). In addition, 11-17 year-olds, experienced higher levels of generalised anxiety during the COVID-19 pandemic (24%) compared with before the pandemic (15%). However, the prevalence of depressive symptoms did not change. In the Netherlands, worse average scores on scales measuring Anger, Peer Relationships, Global health, Sleep-related Impairment, Anxiety, and Depressive Symptoms were recorded among 8-18 year-olds during the period of lockdown (data collected between 10 April and 5 May 2020) than before among children and adolescents of similar ages surveyed in 2018. However the proportions of children manifesting severe symptoms were relatively low and, with the exception of severe Anxiety (17% during lockdown compared to 9% before) and severe Sleep-Related Impairment (12% compared to 6%) were unchanged or slighly lower during lockdown than before (Luijten et al., 2021[6]) (Figure 4.2 below).

Figure 4.1. Likelihood of a mental disorder, 5-16 year-olds, England, 2017 and July 2020 (%)

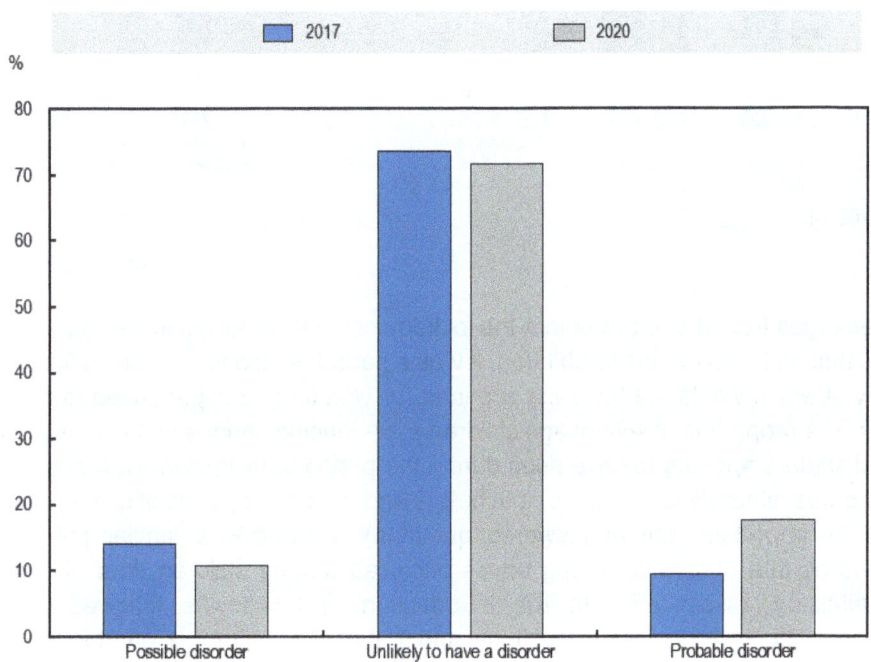

Source: (NHS Digital, 2020[1], Table 1.1).

StatLink https://stat.link/ktn70e

Figure 4.2. Incidence of mental and social health problems in children (8-18 years) and adolescents before and during the COVID-19 lockdown: the Netherlands

Percentage of respondents with poor functioning or severe symptoms

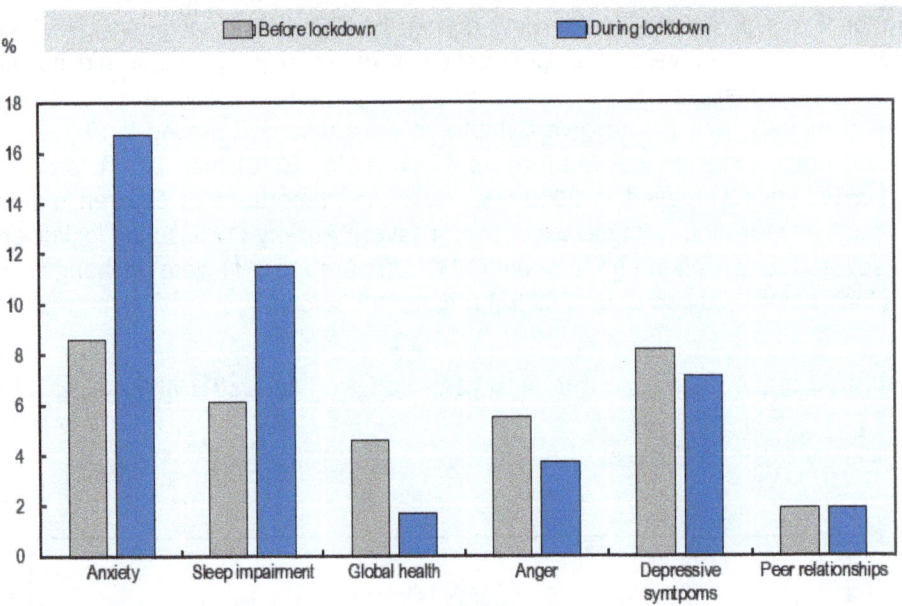

Source: (Luijten et al., 2021[6]).

StatLink ⟶ https://stat.link/bhg07a

The picture that emerges from the above is that the lockdowns and school closures had a range of negative aspects for many, though by no means all children. It was a period of inconvenience, difficulties and stresses for children, many of which would not have experienced (or would have experienced to a lesser degree) in normal conditions. The proportion of school age children experiencing serious or severe symptoms of mental or psychological disorders appears to have risen during the period of lockdown. However, the proportion of children concerned was relatively small. Most, both before and during the period of lockdowns, did not display such symptoms. An important (but unanswered question) is whether a similar pattern of change in psychological state as that observed among adults occurred among children: that of a sharp decline in psychological well-being associated with the introduction of lockdowns followed by a subsequent improvement as with the reduction of restrictions and habituation with the pandemic situation and its consequences.

Home learning: Parents', teachers and students' perceptions

Did the arrangements put in place to support home learning during school closures allow children to maintain their link with schools and teachers and to continue to learn effectively? Two main types of information relevant to this question exist. First, there is the perception of the actors involved', principally parents and to a lesser extent students and teachers. Second, there are a small number of studies that have compared results on standardised tests for students in the cohorts affected by the pandemic with results for students in the same tests in previous years. Information on the perceptions of the actors involved is presented before presenting the results of testing programmes.

The views of parents

How satisfied were parents with the home schooling experience and the support offered by schools and how did they assess the impact of the period of home schooling on children's learning and social development? Table 4.1 summarises the views of parents in France, Germany, Ireland, the United Kingdom and the United States. Overall, parents/guardians had mixed views. Satisfaction with the efforts made by schools and teachers during the period of school closures was balanced by concerns regarding their children's educational progress and, in some cases, their broader social development.

Table 4.1. Parents' views regarding their children's schooling and educational progress during lockdowns

	Country	Children concerned	Aspect of schooling	% of parents
Overall satisfaction	France	Lower secondary school students	Strongly or somewhat in agreement that the activities offered by teachers during the period of school closures had been beneficial to their children	81
		Upper secondary school students (general)		75
	Germany	Primary and secondary education students	Very or moderately happy with school activities during school closure	56
			Very or moderately happy with school teaching during the pandemic	54
	United Kingdom	Dependent child(ren) aged 5 to 18 years living in the household	Agree that the children/child within the household are continuing to learn whilst being home schooled	70
	United States	K-12 students whose children's school is currently closed	Very/somewhat satisfied with the way their children's school handled instruction during the school closure (1)	83
		Children in elementary, middle and high schools that are closed	Satisfied with how much children are learning. (Strongly agree/agree) (2)	64
			Satisfied with the communication to support learning from child's/children's school (Strongly agree/agree) (2)	76
Student progress	France	Secondary school students	Very much/somewhat in agreement that the level of the students learning had been maintained	66
			Very much/somewhat in agreement that the child had progressed in his/her studies	41
			Very much/somewhat in agreement that the level of the child had improved in certain subjects	37
	Germany	Primary and secondary students	Very much/somewhat in agreement that child learnt much less than usual	64
			School has slowed down	34
	Ireland	Primary school children	Major or moderate negative impact of enforced school closures on primary school children's learning	41
			Major or moderate negative impact of enforced school closures on primary school children's social development	42
		Secondary school children	Major or moderate negative impact of enforced school closures on secondary school children's learning	46
			Major or moderate negative impact of enforced school closures on secondary school children's social development	43
			Concerned about about child returning to school because of falling behind during lockdown	36
	United Kingdom	Dependent child aged 5 to 18 years living in the household and who had been home schooled by their parent(s) in the previous 7 days	Oldest or only child struggling to continue education remotely	42

Country	Children concerned	Aspect of schooling	% of parents
United States	K-12 students whose school is currently closed Children in elementary, middle and high school that have been closed	Very/somewhat concerned about child/ren falling behind in school as a result of any disruptions caused by the coronavirus outbreak (1)	64
		Very/somewhat likely that school closures due to the Coronavirus pandemic will lead child to not make as much progress academically (2)	34
		Child/children will be prepared for school in the next school year (strongly agree or agree) (2)	74
	K-12 students	Very or moderately concerned that the coronavirus situation will have a negative impact on child's education (3)	42

Sources: France: (Direction de l'évaluation de la prospective et de la performance (DEPP), 2020[2], Figure 9-3); Germany: (D21 Initiative/TUM/Kantar, 2020[12]; Wößmann et al., 2020[13]); Ireland: (Central Statistics Office (CSO), 2020[14]); United Kingdom: (Office for National Statistics (ONS), 2020[11]); United States: (1) (Horowitz, 2020[15]); (2) (University of Southern California (USC), 2020[16]); (3) (Brenan, 2020[17]).

In terms of an overall appreciation of the work of teachers and schools during school closures, a large majority of parents in France, the United Kingdom and the United States expressed satisfaction. High proportions of parents of secondary school students in France agreed that the activities offered by teachers during the period of school closures had been beneficial to their children (75% to 81% depending on their level of schooling). The amount of work that gave to their children was seen as appropriate by nearly two out of three parents of secondary school students with between 17% and 23% of parents seeing it as being too much and between 12% and 20% as too little (depending on the educational level) (Direction de l'évaluation de la prospective et de la performance (DEPP), 2020[2], Figure 2-11). Four out of five US parents (83%) reported being satisfied with the way their children's school had been handling instruction during school closures and 64% were satisfied with how much their children were learning. In addition, high proportions of US parents expressed satisfaction with the communication with their child(ren)'s school (Jones, 2020[18]; University of Southern California (USC), 2020[16]).[3]

The levels of satisfaction of German parents were lower than in the other three countries. However, the majority were satisfied. Some 54% of German parents were moderately or very satisfied with the school lessons of their children during the pandemic, feeling that schools had done "all that was in their power" (59%) and acknowledging that teachers transformed their teaching on their own initiative (54%). At the same time, 33% were moderately or very unsatisfied overall, with 42% finding that teachers were overwhelmed with the digital transformation of their teaching and 24% that schools went at a slower pace (D21 Initiative/TUM/Kantar, 2020[12]). Another study found similar results: 56% of parents reported being very or rather satisfied with school activities during school closures and 38% reported being very or rather dissatisfied (Wößmann et al., 2020[13]).

Figure 4.3. Opinions of parents regarding the instructional activities offered to their children by teachers, by child's level of schooling: France (%)

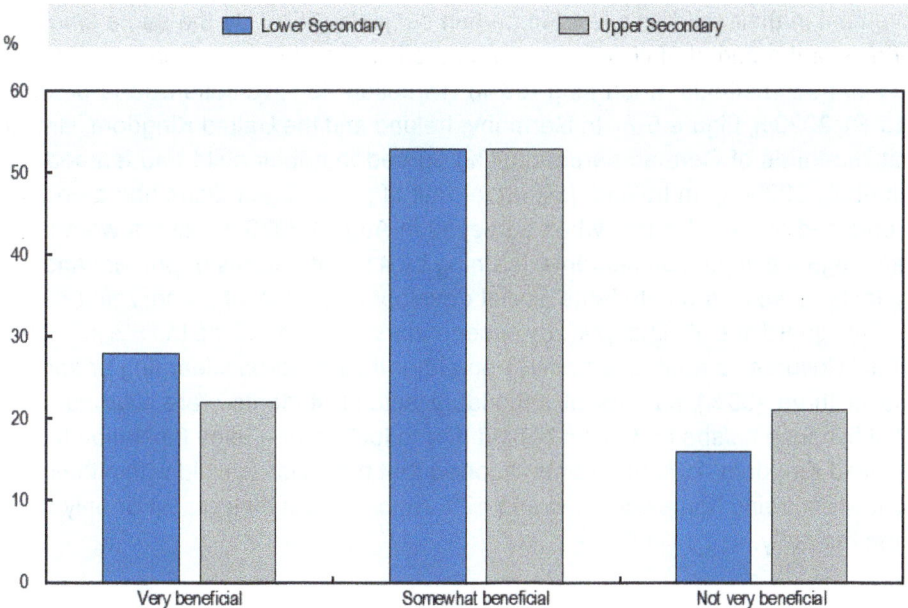

Source: (Direction de l'évaluation de la prospective et de la performance (DEPP), 2020[2], Figures 4-5 and 4-6).

StatLink https://stat.link/1hqxs7

Figure 4.4. Level of satisfaction of parents of K-12 children with the way children's school has been handling instruction during the school closure: United States, April 2020

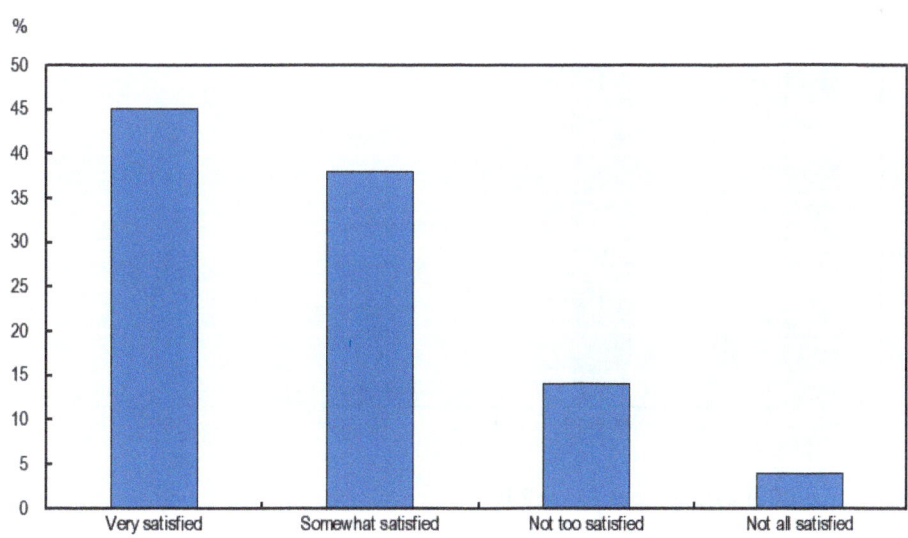

Source: (Horowitz, 2020[15])

StatLink https://stat.link/pbt5fg

Parents were, however, generally less satisfied with their children's learning and academic progress. Only 66% of French parents of secondary school students strongly or somewhat agreed that their children's learning had been maintained and far fewer were in agreement that it had progressed (39%) or that there had been improvement in their children's level in certain subjects (35%). At the same time, French parents noted positive effects of the period of closures such as the increased independence of their children (57%) and the discovery of new methods of learning (56%) (Direction de l'évaluation de la prospective et de la performance (DEPP), 2020[2], Figure 5-7). In Germany, Ireland and the United Kingdom, similar results were observed. Almost two-thirds of German parents (64%) agreed that their child had learned much less than usual (Wößmann et al., 2020[13]). In Ireland, just under half of parents/guardians had a negative perception of the impact of enforced school closures when surveyed in August 2020. Closures were seen as having a major or moderate negative impact on students' learning by 41% of parents of primary and 46% of parents of secondary students as well as on students' social development (42% of primary and 43% of secondary parents). Few parents/guardians of either primary or secondary students (close to 15% in both cases) viewed the impact of school closures as neutral or positive on either their children's learning or social development (Figure 4.5). One in three (36%) parents of secondary school students were worried about their child returning to school because he/she had fallen behind due to lockdown (Office for National Statistics (ONS), 2020[11]). In the United Kingdom, 70% of parents reported that the children/child within their household were continuing to learn whilst being home schooled and 42% reported that their oldest or only child struggled to continue education remotely.

Figure 4.5. Parents' views of the impact of enforced school closures on children's learning by level of schooling: Ireland, August 2020

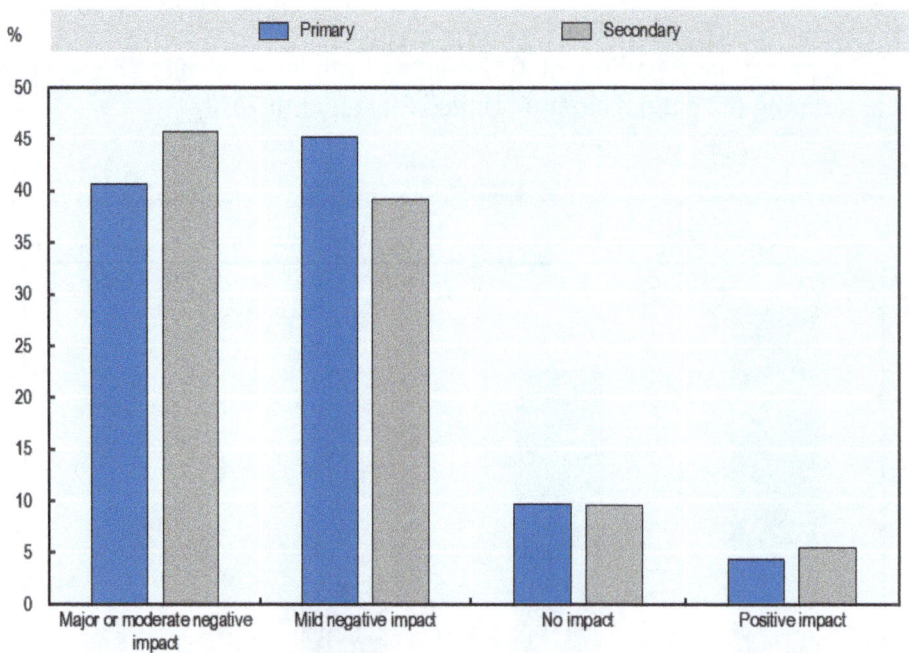

Source: (Central Statistics Office (CSO), 2020[14], Tables 2.1 and 2.4).

StatLink https://stat.link/qspj7x

Figure 4.6. Parents' views regarding the likelihood that the COVID-19 pandemic will lead to their child not making as much progress academically (% by category), United States, May 2020

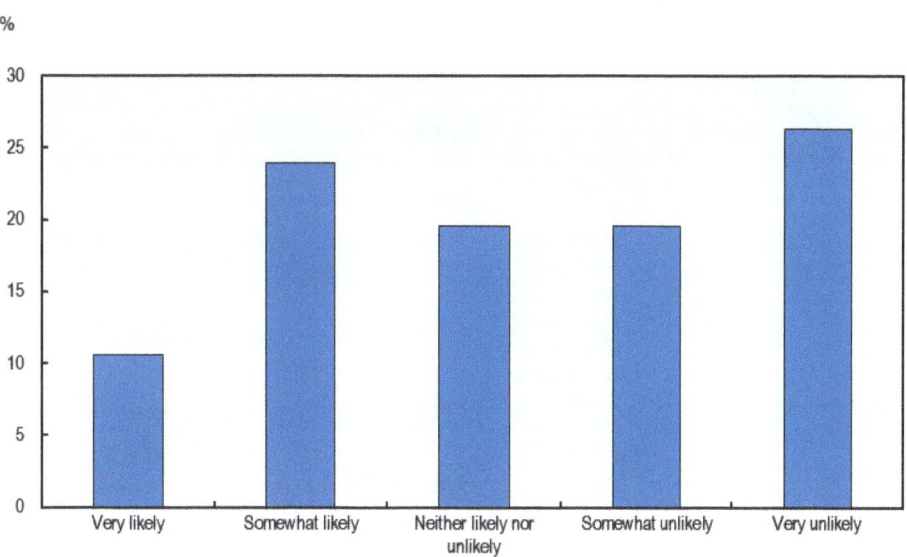

Source: (University of Southern California (USC), 2020[16]).

StatLink https://stat.link/6t4xgh

Evidence regarding US parents' assessment of the likely impact of school closures on their children's educational progress is mixed with between one-third to two-thirds of parents expressing concerns. In late March 2020, less than half (42%) of parents of K-12 students were "very" or "moderately" concerned that the pandemic would have a negative impact on their child's education. A poll conducted in early April 2020, reported less positive opinions: 64% of parents were concerned about their children falling behind as a result of the Coronavirus outbreak. However, in May in another survey (University of Southern California (USC), 2020[16]), US parents were more positive: only 34% of parents thought it somewhat or very likely that their child would not make as much progress academically due to school closures (Figure 4.6) and 74% agreed that their child(ren) would be well prepared for school in the next school year.

The evidence regarding the relationship between concerns regarding the negative impact of lockdowns and school closures on children's academic progress is mixed (Table 4.2). No relationship between views of the impact of closures on student progress and parental education or income is seen in the Irish and UK data. In France, the satisfaction of parents was only weakly related to their socio-economic status. Views regarding the benefits of the activities provided to children were unrelated to social background, but advantaged parents were slightly more satisfied with their children's progress than their less advantaged peers. In the United States, the existence and direction of an association between parental views regarding the impacts of closures on their children's academic progress and parental education, income or race varies between studies.

Table 4.2. The relationship between socio-economic background and parental concerns regarding the academic progress of children

France, Ireland, the United Kingdom and the United States

	France	Ireland	United Kingdom	United States		
	DEPP	CSO	ONS	Brenan	Horowitz	USC
Parental education	n/a	n/a	Primary students – no relationship. Secondary students - parents with less than degree level education more likely to report negative impact	No relationship	n/a	n/a	No relationship
Parental income	n/a	n/a	n/a	No relationship	n/a	Low income parents more likely to report concerns than middle or upper income parents	No relationship
Parental socio-economic status	No relationship	Low status parents slightly more likely to state that their child had not progressed	n/a	n/a	n/a	n/a	n/a
Parental race/ethnic background	n/a	n/a	n/a	n/a	Non-whites more concerned than whites	n/a	No relationship
Data item	Activities provided for children in secondary school were very or moderately beneficial	Moderately or very much in agreement that their child had advanced in his/her learning	Major or moderate negative impact on child's learning	Oldest or only child in the home struggling to continue to their education while at home	Very/moderately concerned that the coronavirus situation will have a negative impact on child's education	Very/somewhat concerned about child/ren falling behind in school as a result of disruptions caused by the Coronavirus outbreak	Very/somewhat likely that school closures due to the Coronavirus pandemic will lead child to not make as much progress academically

Sources: France: (Direction de l'évaluation, de la prospective et de la performance (DEPP), 2020[19]); Ireland: (Central Statistics Office (CSO), 2020[14]); United Kingdom: (Office for National Statistics (ONS), 2020[11]); United States: (Brenan, 2020[17]; Horowitz, 2020[15]; University of Southern California (USC), 2020[16]).

The views of students and teachers

Unfortunately, in most countries, little information is available regarding the views of pupils or teachers regarding the utility and effectiveness of home-based schooling during the period of school closures. An exception is France where information is available on the views of students, teachers and school principals.

Just under two-thirds of French secondary school pupils (63-64% depending on the type of school) felt that the *quantity* of school work that they were asked to do was appropriate with around a third considering that it was too great and 4-7% too little (Direction de l'évaluation de la prospective et de la performance (DEPP), 2020[2], Figure 2-12). In a poll conducted in the United States in late July/early August 2020, 46% of school students in grades 3-12 reported that they believed that they would have to catch up in the coming school year because of the time spent learning from home in the spring of 2020 (Marken and Clayton, 2020[20]).

A large majority of school teachers in France were of the view that their students had learnt in a satisfactory or highly satisfactory manner during the period of school closures. This was true of 77% of primary school teachers and 68% of secondary teachers (Direction de l'évaluation de la prospective et de la performance (DEPP), 2020[2], Figures 1-1 and 1-2). In addition, most secondary teachers considered the arrangements put in place during school closures to have had (to a large or to some extent) a positive influence on the acquisition of digital skills (80%) and on the autonomy of pupils (78%). In contrast, few considered that these arrangements had a positive impact on either the reduction of inequalities (10%) or the motivation of pupils regarding their schooling (38%) (Direction de l'évaluation de la prospective et de la performance (DEPP), 2020[2], Figure 9-2).

School principals in France offered a broadly similar evaluation to teachers with 74% of primary principals and between 67% and 84% (according to the type of school) of the senior management in secondary schools considering that their students had learnt in a satisfactory or highly satisfactory manner during the period of school closures (Direction de l'évaluation de la prospective et de la performance (DEPP), 2020[2], Figure 1-1). Reflecting this, only a quarter of French primary school principals felt that the level of proficiency in reading (26%) and in mathematics (calculation and number) (24%) was lower for most or all pupils enrolled in year 2 at the start of the 2020-21 school than was the case for pupils in the same grade at the start of the previous school year (Direction de l'évaluation, de la prospective et de la performance (DEPP), 2021[21], Figure 2).

Evidence from standardised achievement tests

To what extent are the concerns of parents that their children's academic progress was negatively affected during the period of school closures supported by actual evidence regarding student performance? Potential sources of empirical information regarding the academic progress of pupils affected by closures can come from: (1) comparisons of the academic performance of the same students before and after (or during) the period of school closures; (2) comparisons of students in given years who experienced disruption to their education with cohorts of in the same years of schooling in previous years. Unfortunately, due to the pandemic, most countries suspended national testing programmes in the 2019-20 school year. Few data are available, therefore, that permit an evaluation of the immediate effect of the school closures of March-June 2020 on the achievement of the pupils concerned (i.e. data collected during or within 6 months following immediately the period of closures).

Description of the available data

Relevant data are available, nevertheless, in a number of countries and several comparisons of the performance of students experiencing school closures in the first half of 2020 with students in the same year of schooling in 2019 and earlier years have been published. These include results from national or provincial level testing programmes (Baden-Württemberg, France, Italy and the Netherlands) and system-specific testing programmes (Catholic schools in Flanders). Data from online tests used in schools (England, Switzerland and the United States) has also been analysed as have results from smaller scale studies designed to examine the impact of school closures on student performance (Australia, England).

In assessing the strength of the available evidence regarding the impact of school closures during the first half of 2020 on the performance of school children, it is important to note the considerable differences between studies. They differ in terms of their design (especially in the nature of samples), the year groups covered, and rates of participation by schools and by pupils in tests conducted in 2020/21. Table 4.3 provides a summary of the characteristics of the data and analysis used in the different studies.[4] Of the studies reviewed, those from Australia, Flanders, France, Germany (Baden-Württemberg) and Italy are based on censuses or representative samples (with the Flemish tests having very low rates of participation of schools in the 2020 testing round). The remainder are based on non-representative or convenience samples of various kinds involving a degree of self-selection by participating schools[5] and/or pupils – e.g. schools that use a particular (proprietary) test, volunteer schools, etc.

The type of information on performance also varies. Some studies assess *growth* in performance in the 2020 school year (i.e. change in performance between different measurement points in the 2020 school year) compared to the change observed among similar pupils in previous years. Others compare *performance levels*, i.e. the performance of a grade cohort (e.g. year 6 students) at the end of the 2020 school year or in the course of the 2021 school year with the performance of the same year cohort in previous years. The statistics used to report performance also vary. Where possible, differences in scaled scores have been standardised as a proportion of a standard deviation (SD) to help comparison if this has not already been done by the authors of the studies concerned.

In addition, the dates at which the tests were administered vary and with this, the interval of time that has elapsed between the first wave of school closures and the conduct of the assessment. This needs to be taken into account when interpreting (and comparing) the results. The results of tests taken during or soon after the March-June 2020 period of closures, in addition to cumulated learning to that point, will reflect primarily the impact of these closures. However, the results of testing undertaken at later dates will reflect a range of additional influences. These include: disruptions to schooling in the 2020-21 school year (including any further school closures or lockdowns), the effects of measures taken by schools to consolidate the instruction which pupils did not fully cover in the 2019-20 school year as well as any action taken by students and their families to make up for any missed instruction (e.g. additional after-school tuition). For the most part, the results presented in Table 4.3 come from tests administered either during or within six months of the end of the first wave of school closures. The exception is the Italian assessments which were administered in May 2021 and which, therefore, are far more affected by experience of pupils following the first wave of school closures than the others. Finally, the assessments may also vary in terms of their objectives and purposes.

In terms of coverage of students in the grade levels tested, the best data concerning the academic progress of the cohort of students affected by school closures come from France, the German Länder of Baden-Württemberg, Italy and Ohio in the United States. Both the French and Italian assessments are national assessments covering students in public and private schools. The Baden-Württemberg assessments cover students in public schools and the Ohio assessment covers pupils in all primary schools in the state. In all, the participation rates among the target populations are high.

Findings concerning academic achievement and progress

The results reported in the available studies vary considerably. Improvement, as well as stability and decline in the performance of the "COVID cohorts" relative to their peers tested in previous years is observed (Table 4.4). There are no clear patterns within or between countries or by learning area (e.g. reading/language compared to mathematics). In the studies presented, performance in mathematics declines as opposed to remaining unchanged or improving more frequently than does performance in tests of language skills (e.g. reading in the national language). However, even in the case of mathematics, cases of no change and improvement are observed.

An important question is how to evaluate the scale of the observed differences in the academic achievement of the COVID cohorts with cohorts in previous years. What is a "large" and what is a "small" difference? Expressing the differences in terms of the normal performance gain over a given time period is one way of doing this. This is undertaken in a number of the studies presented. However, variation in the basis of the calculations, particularly assumptions regarding normal achievement gain mean that the comparisons should be made with caution. The big challenge is estimating what range of growth in performance would be expected over a year in "normal" conditions. A range of benchmarks have been proposed, from 0.25 of a standard deviation in test scores (Avvisati and Givord, 2021[22], based on the Programme for International Student Assessment [PISA]) to 0.65 (Schult et al., 2021[23]).[6] These depend, to some extent, on the particular studies, the country and the grade group concerned.

Whatever the benchmark used, the falls in performance reported in Flanders (particularly in Dutch language) and, to a lesser degree, in Italy at secondary level (final year of high school) in Italian and mathematics seem very large. For example, the reported fall in the performance of year 6 students in 2020 relative to students in previous years in Dutch language (-0.3 SD) in Flanders represents the equivalent of between 50%-75% of the estimated average achievement gain in a normal school year depending on the benchmark used. The decline in scores in Italian among Year 13 students represents between 40% and 60% of "normal" annual gain.

In particular, the scale of the declines found in Flanders seem implausible. They imply that the substitution of remote schooling for school-based instruction for a period of seven weeks[7] (around 20% of yearly instruction time) meant that the improvement in achievement of Year 5 students in Dutch was between 25%-50% of what it would have been in a "normal" year. At the same time, the estimates of a performance decline equivalent to around two to three months of usual annual learning gain found in the Dutch and English studies suggest that, at best, students maintained the level of performance they had achieved when their schools closed. This again seems surprising given that most students continued some form of school learning from home during school closures.

The results that suggest no impact of the disruption to schooling on performance also raise questions. In particular, they stand in contrast with the evidence that even if most pupils continued with their education, they spent less time, on average, in learning activities than they would have done in a normal year.

An important issue that is not addressed in any detail by the studies reviewed is that of the variation observed in the results of testing programmes over time prior to 2020. Placing the results of COVID cohorts in the context of longer run trends (where they exist) is instructive (see Figures 4.7 and 4.8). As can be seen, the magnitude of the changes in performance observed between 2019 and 2020 in Baden-Württemberg and in France is within the range of what has been observed in the recent past. Importantly, falls as well as increases in performance are also observed in previous years.[8] The main point to be drawn from this is that care should be exercised in making causal inferences regarding the effect of school closures on academic performance on the basis of observed changes in performance between 2020 and 2019 alone.

Figure 4.7. Mean scores in reading and mathematics: Year 5 pupils, Baden-Württemberg, 2015-2020

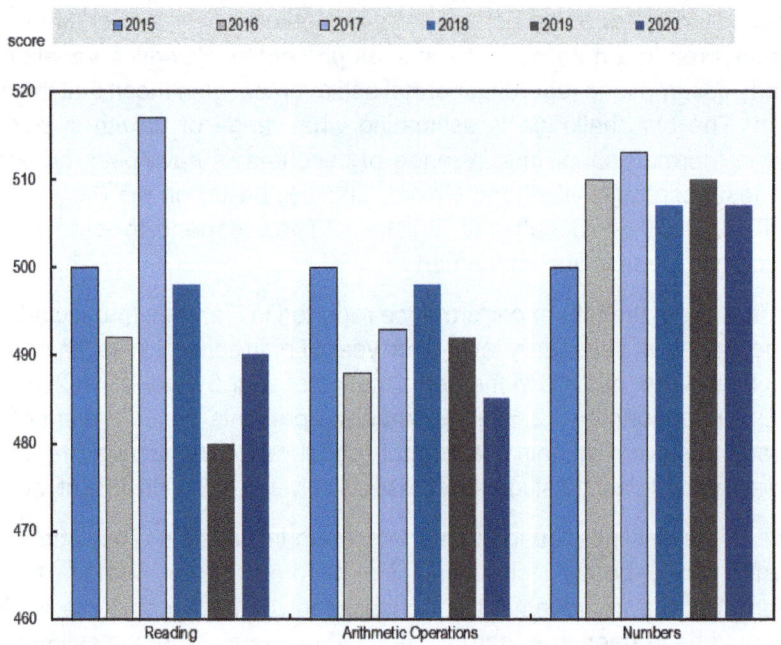

Source: (Schult et al., 2021[23], Table 2).

StatLink https://stat.link/stzup8

Figure 4.8. Proportion of Year 6 pupils with satisfactory or better mastery of French and Mathematics: France, 2017-2020

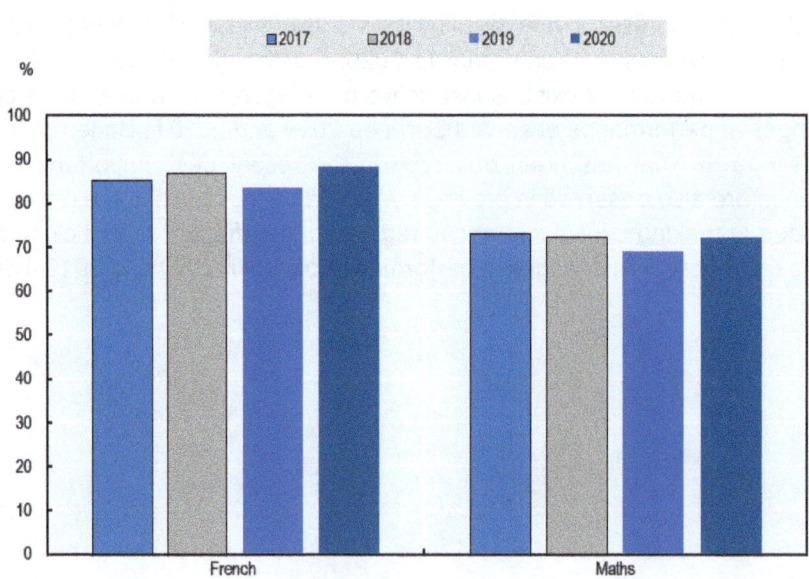

Source: (Direction de l'évaluation, de la prospective et de la performance (DEPP), 2020[24], Figures 3.3.1 and 3.3.2).

StatLink https://stat.link/720kfb

Evidence regarding the differential impact of the disruptions to education caused by school closures by socio-economic background is also mixed. Several studies find little evidence of change in the performance gaps related to social background. Others find increases[9] and in a few cases declines (for some year groups in some subjects). In countries in which results are available for pupils in several year levels in different subjects, the extent and direction of change in performance gaps related to socio-economic background can vary by year and subject (e.g. France and Italy).

The variation in the results found between studies is intriguing and its explanation is beyond the scope of this report. The experience of lockdowns and school closures may have varied considerably between countries and regions depending on the severity of restrictions and the nature of teaching and support for learning provided to schoolchildren. Apart from issues of sampling, the timing of testing and missing data mentioned above, the conditions in which the tests were administered is also relevant. Assessments administered during March-June 2020 were conducted in conditions of considerable disruption to normal schooling arrangements. This was less true of tests administered in September at the start of the 2021-22 school year (especially in Europe). The extent to which tests conducted later in the 2021-22 school year took place in relatively "normal" conditions depends on the country concerned. In France, for example, schools remained open over the 2021-22 school year whereas in other countries (e.g. Italy) further episodes of closures occurred or schools remained closed for much of the year (e.g. many States in the United States). In addition, the extent to which the tests evaluate knowledge directly related to the content of the curriculum may differ. For example, the German and French assessments are primarily diagnostic in focus rather than intended to evaluate what had been learnt in the previous year. It is possible that performance on tests that focus on more "generic" content and procedural knowledge are less affected than those focusing on specific curriculum content by the changes to the mode and content of instruction during school closures. Closures, for example, may have meant that pupils covered some of the content tested in assessments designed to evaluate the mastery of curricular knowledge and skills either incompletely or not at all. The risk of this is far less in assessments designed to assess more general or generic skills and knowledge.

Table 4.3. Methodological features of comparisons of the academic performance of COVID cohorts with pre-COVID cohorts

	Test	Grades covered	Date of testing of COVID cohort	Sample	Participation rate of schools in 2020 or 2021 tests	Participation rate of students in 2020/21	Method	Reference
Australia	ACER Progressive Achievement Tests in mathematics, reading and science	Years 3 and 4	January-April and October-December 2020	Pupils in Years 3 and 4 in Government primary schools in New South Wales (62 schools in 2019 and 51 schools in 2020)	n/a	n/a	Comparisons of achievement growth between term 1 and term 4 in the 2019 and 2020 school years.	(Gore et al., 2021[25])
England	NFER assessments	Year 2	November 2020	Volunteer sample of 168 primary schools	n/a	No information provided	Comparison of 2020 sample with "benchmark values" from 2017 standardisation sample.	(Rose et al., 2021[26])
	Renaissance Learning's Star Reading and Star Maths Assessments	Years 3-9	Early and late autumn 2020	Students taking Star Reading and Star Mathematics assessments tested in both autumn 2019 and autumn 2020	n/a	n/a	Comparison of "actual" progress between autumn 2019 and autumn 2020 with "expected" progress for students with results at both points.	(Renaissance Learning, Education Policy Institute, 2021[27])
Flanders	Standardised tests used in the Catholic school system	Year 6	June 2020	All Catholic primary schools in Flanders	27%	No information provided	Comparisons with results from equivalent tests in previous years (2015 to 2019), with and without controls.	(Maldonado and De Witte, 2021[28])
France	Repères CP, CE1 (national assessments)	Years 1 and 2	September 2020	All public and private primary schools	100%	97%	Comparisons with results from equivalent tests in previous years (2018 and 2019).	DEPP (2020[29])
	Point d'étape CP (national assessment)	Year 1	January 2021	All public and private primary schools	99%	99%	Comparisons with results from equivalent tests in previous years (2018 and 2019).	DEPP (2021[30])
	Évaluation de début de sixième (national assessment)	Year 6	September 2020	All public and private lower secondary schools (collèges)	97%	93% - French language 94% - mathematics	Comparisons with results from equivalent tests in previous years (2017, 2018 and 2019).	DEPP (2020[24])

	Test	Grades covered	Date of testing of COVID cohort	Sample	Participation rate of schools in 2020 or 2021 tests	Participation rate of students in 2020/21	Method	Reference
Germany	Standardised reading comprehension and mathematics tests	Year 5	September 2020	Public schools with Year 5 students in Baden-Württemberg	Not specified	Not specified	Comparisons with the average of results for previous three years (2017 to 2019) of year 5 students. Results for the individual years 2015-19 also presented.	(Schult et al., 2021[23])
Italy	Standardised national tests (INVALSI)	Year 2	May 2021	All primary and secondary schools	Not specified	98%	Comparisons with results for students in the same grade in 2019.	(INVALSI, 2021[31])
		Year 5	May 2021			98%		
		Year 8	May 2021			93%		
		Year 13	May 2021			82%		
Netherlands	National assessments (mathematics, spelling and reading)	Years 4-7	June 2020	Schools in a dataset covering students in 15% of Dutch primary schools throughout the years 2017–2020.	n/a	43-65% of students participated in both mid- and end-year tests depending on their age and the test domain	Comparison of growth between end-year and mid-year assessments for 2020 compared with estimates combining three previous years (2017, 2018 and 2019) with controls.	(Engzell, Frey and Verhagen, 2020[32])
United States	MAP assessments	Years 3-8	Autumn 2020	US Public schools using MAP assessments that tested at least ten students in a given grade in both fall 2019 and fall 2020.	n/a	75% in reading 74% in maths	Comparison of levels and growth in performance for students tested in 2020 with that of students tested in 2019.	(Johnson and Kuhfeld, 2020[33]), (Kuhfeld et al., 2020[34])
	Ohio English Language Arts Assessment	Year 3	Autumn 2020	All Grade 3 pupils in primary schools in Ohio	Not specified	81%	Comparison of levels and growth in performance for students tested in 2020 with that of students tested in 2019	(Kogan and Lavertu, 2021[35])

Table 4.4. Academic performance of COVID cohorts compared to peers in previous years

Country	Grades tested	Subjects tested	Achievement of COVID cohorts compared with that of similar students in previous years		Comparison group/benchmark	Change in the scale of performance gaps by socio-economic background	Strength of evidence
			Change in level	Change in growth			
Australia (New South Wales)	Year 3	Reading		no change	Students at the same grade level in matched schools in 2019		++++
		Maths		no change			
	Year 4	Reading		no change			
		Maths		no change			
England (NFER)	Year 2	Reading	-0.17 SD		2017 "standardisation" sample	Achievement gaps reported to widen for disadvantaged students	+
		Mathematics	-0.14 SD				
England (Renaissance)	Year 3	Reading		-1.8 months	'Expected growth' based on results for pupils in the same school years in 2017-19	Performance declines are greater for students from disadvantaged backgrounds in both reading and mathematics	+++
	Year 4	Reading		-1.8 months			
	Year 5	Reading		-1.9 months			
	Year 6	Reading		-2.0 months			
	Year 7	Reading		-0.9 months			
	Year 8	Reading		-1.6 months			
	Year 9	Reading		-2.0 months			
	Primary	Maths		-3.2 months			
Flanders	Year 6	Dutch	-0.29 SD		Students in the same year group in 2019. (Results also available for comparisons with students in the same year over 2015-2019 depending on subject)	Learning losses found to increase with the share of students in schools with low socioeconomic status	+++
		Mathematics	-0.19 SD				
		Social Science	-0.07 SD (ns)				
		French	-0.30 SD				
		Science	-0.33 SD				

Country	Grades tested	Subjects tested	Achievement of COVID cohorts compared with that of similar students in previous years		Comparison group/benchmark	Change in the scale of performance gaps by socio-economic background	Strength of evidence
			Change in level	Change in growth			
France	Year 1 (start of year)	French*	-0.9 to +2.5 percentage points in % of pupils above threshold		Pupils in the same grade undertaking the assessment in 2019	Performance gaps between schools with high proportions of disadvantaged students and other schools increase slightly with greatest increase for students in Year 2	+++++
		Mathematics*	-1.7 to -0.7 percentage points in % of pupils above threshold				
	Year 2 (start of year)	French*	-1.7 to -0.7 percentage points in % of pupils above threshold				
		Mathematics*	-4.8 to +0.4 percentage points in % of pupils above threshold				
	Year 6 (start of year)	French	+4.8 percentage points in % of pupils above threshold			Performance gaps between advantaged and disadvantaged schools decline for French and increase slightly in maths	
		Mathematics	+3.0 percentage points in % of pupils above threshold				
	Year 1 (mid-year)	French*	+1.4 to +1.9 percentage points in % of pupils above threshold		Pupils in the same grade undertaking the assessment in 2020	Performance gaps between advantaged and disadvantaged schools increase slightly in French and maths	
		Mathematics*	+2.0 percentage points in % of pupils above threshold				

Country	Grades tested	Subjects tested	Achievement of COVID cohorts compared with that of similar students in previous years		Comparison group/benchmark	Change in the scale of performance gaps by socio-economic background	Strength of evidence
			Change in level	Change in growth			
Germany (Baden-Württemberg)	Year 5	Reading	-0.07 SD		Average performance of year 5 students in similar tests over the three previous years (2017-2019)	School characteristics such as the average socio-cultural capital and the proportion of students with migration background did not show substantial relationships with schools' competence change scores	+++++
		Number (Maths)	-0.09 SD				
		Operations (Maths)	-0.03 SD				
Italy	Year 2	Italian	+0.12 SD		Performance of students in the same grades in 2019	No information	+++++
		Maths	-0.06 SD (ns)				
	Year 5	Italian	+0.13 SD			No information	
		Maths	-0.07 SD (ns)				
		English (reading)	+0.03 SD (ns)				
		English (listening)	+0.01 SD (ns)				
	Year 8	Italian	-0.08 SD			Increase in the share of students in difficulty in Italian is greatest for students from low socio-economic status (SES) background. The reverse true for maths.	
		Maths	-0.18 SD				
		English (reading)	-0.00 SD (ns)				
		English (listening)	+0.00 SD (ns)				
	Year 13	Italian	-0.25 SD			Increase in the share of students in difficulty in Italian and maths is greatest for students from low SES backgrounds	
		Maths	-0.24 SD				
		English (reading)	-0.06 SD (ns)				
		English (listening)	+0.05 SD (ns)				
Netherlands	Years 4-7	Composite scale combining mathematics, spelling and reading		-0.08 SD	Estimated growth between end-year and mid-year assessments for pupils undertaking assessments in 2017 to 2019	Learning losses found to be up to 60% larger among students from less-educated homes	+++

Country	Grades tested	Subjects tested	Achievement of COVID cohorts compared with that of similar students in previous years		Comparison group/benchmark	Change in the scale of performance gaps by socio-economic background	Strength of evidence
			Change in level	Change in growth			
United States (MAPS)	Year 3	Reading	0 percentile pts	-1 percentile pts	Students tested in 2019	No evidence for achievement gaps increasing by race. Some evidence for increasing gaps by poverty level of school	++++
		Maths	-9 percentile pts	-9 percentile pts			
	Year 4	Reading	-2 percentile pts	-3 percentile pts			
		Maths	-10 percentile pts	-11 percentile pts			
	Year 5	Reading	-1 percentile pts	-2 percentile pts			
		Maths	-9 percentile pts	-11 percentile pts			
	Year 6	Reading	0 percentile pts	-1 percentile pts			
		Maths	-6 percentile pts	-4 percentile pts			
	Year 7	Reading	+1 percentile pts	-2 percentile pts			
		Maths	-5 percentile pts	-4 percentile pts			
	Year 8	Reading	+1 percentile pts				
		Maths	-6 percentile pts				
United States (Ohio)	Year 3	English language	-0.23 SD		Students in the same grade tested in 2019	Falls in scores for Black students were nearly 50% larger than for White students. The scores of economically disadvantaged students fell more than those of other students	+++++

Note: (ns) not statistically significant.
* The French language and maths tests cover several domains that are reported separately. The threshold level is that of "satisfactory performance" or higher ("maîtrise satisfaisante" or "très bonne maîtrise").

Sources: Australia: (Gore et al., 2021[25]); England: (Rose et al., 2021[26]), (Renaissance Learning, Education Policy Institute, 2021[27]); Flanders: (Maldonado and De Witte, 2021[28]); France: (Direction de l'évaluation, de la prospective et de la performance (DEPP), 2020[29]; 2021[30]); Germany: (Schult et al., 2021[23]); Italy: (INVALSI, 2021[31]); the Netherlands: (Engzell, Frey and Verhagen, 2020[32]); United States: (Johnson and Kuhfeld, 2020[33]; Kuhfeld et al., 2020[34]; Kogan and Lavertu, 2021[35]).

In the final analysis, time will be needed before it is possible to gain a comprehensive understanding of the short- and long-run consequences of the period of school closures during the first wave of the pandemic on the achievement and broader development of students. Placing the results for 2020 in the context of longer run trends is essential for their interpretation and the next waves of testing programmes will provide vital information. For the moment, considerable caution should be exercised in attributing a causal relationship between the disruption to children's education due to lockdowns and school closures and differences in the performance in standardised assessments of students in a given grade tested in 2020 and 2021 compared to that off students in the same grade(s) tested in previous years. Many factors can lead to variations in performance between different cohorts at the same point in their schooling: different educational experiences, variation in their demographic characteristics and social composition, measurement errors (including variation in test content and test administration between years), and in the case of sample studies, sampling errors. Quite large variations in the performance of different cohorts in the same jurisdiction are often observed in "normal" conditions in standardised testing programmes[10] without any obvious explanation. Adjustments can be made to account for some of these factors in analysis, but not for others.

Summary

Overall, the period of school closures and wider lockdowns appears to have had some negative effects on the psychological well-being of school students. It was the source of inconveniences, constraints, difficulties and stresses additional to those experienced by children in the normal course of life. The majority of children reported a negative appreciation of the period of lockdown and school closures, particularly the lack of social contacts with friends. The share of school age children experiencing serious or severe symptoms of mental or psychological disorders appears to have risen during the period of lockdown. However, the proportion of children concerned was relatively small. Parents had an overall more positive view of the effects of the lockdowns on their children.

Drawing conclusions regarding the effect of the period of school closures and remote schooling on learning and academic progress is relatively difficult at this point. Among parents, satisfaction with the efforts made by schools and teachers during the period of school closures was balanced by concerns regarding their children's educational progress and, in some cases, on their broader social development. The evidence from achievement tests is mixed. Improvement, as well as stability and decline in the performance of the "COVID cohorts" relative to their peers tested in previous years is observed. Evidence regarding the differential impact of the disruptions to education caused by school closures by socio-economic background is also mixed, with some studies finding performance gaps increased and others finding that gaps remained stable or, in a few cases, were reduced. In some countries, the scale and direction of changes in the associations between test performance and social origin varied by year level and subject.

References

Avvisati, F. and P. Givord (2021), "The learning gain over one school year among 15-year-olds: An analysis of PISA data for Austria and Scotland (United Kingdom)", *OECD Education Working Papers*, No. 249, OECD Publishing, Paris, https://dx.doi.org/10.1787/d99e8c0a-en. [22]

Brenan, M. (2020), *42% of Parents Worry COVID-19 Will Affect Child's Education, Gallup Panel, 24-29 March 2020*, https://news.gallup.com/poll/305819/parents-worry-covid-affect-child-education.aspx. [17]

Central Bureau of Statistics (2020), *Civilian Resilience in Israel and the COVID-19 Pandemic: Analysis of a CBS Survey*, INSS Insight No. 1318, https://www.inss.org.il/publication/coronavirus-survey/. [10]

Central Statistics Office (CSO) (2020), *Social Impact of COVID-19 Survey: The Reopening of Schools*, CSO statistical publication, 27 August 2020, Ireland, https://www.cso.ie/en/releasesandpublications/ep/p-sic19ros/socialimpactofcovid-19surveyaugust2020thereopeningofschools/. [14]

Curriculum Associates (2020), *Understanding Student Needs: Early Results from Fall Assessments*, Research Report No. 2020-49, Curriculum Associates, North Billerica, MA, https://www.curriculumassociates.com/-/media/mainsite/files/i-ready/iready-diagnostic-results-understanding-student-needs-paper-2020.pdf. [39]

D21 Initiative/TUM/Kantar (2020), *Erfolgreiches Homeschooling während Corona*, https://www.kantar.com/de/inspiration/d21/erfolgreiches-homeschooling-waehrend-corona. [12]

Direction de l'évaluation, de la prospective et de la performance (DEPP) (2021), *Dispositif d'évaluation des conséquences de la crise sanitaire : comment les élèves ont-ils vécu le confinement de mars-avril 2020 ?*, Note d'information n°21.19 – Avril, Ministère de l'Education nationale, de la Jeunesse et des Sports, https://www.education.gouv.fr/dispositif-d-evaluation-des-consequences-de-la-crise-sanitaire-comment-les-eleves-ont-ils-vecu-le-322830. [5]

Direction de l'évaluation, de la prospective et de la performance (DEPP) (2021), *Dispositif d'évaluation des conséquences de la crise sanitaire : le point de vue des directeurs et directrices d'école*, Note d'Information n°21.04, Ministère de l'Education nationale, de la Jeunesse et des Sports, https://www.education.gouv.fr/dispositif-d-evaluation-des-consequences-de-la-crise-sanitaire-le-point-de-vue-des-directeurs-et-309164. [21]

Direction de l'évaluation, de la prospective et de la performance (DEPP) (2021), "Évaluations 2021 Point d'étape CP : Premiers résultats", *Série Études*, No. 2021-E03, mars 2021, Ministère de l'Education nationale, de la Jeunesse et des Sports, Paris, https://www.education.gouv.fr/evaluations-2021-point-d-etape-cp-premiers-resultats-322673. [30]

Direction de l'évaluation, de la prospective et de la performance (DEPP) (2020), *Confinement : un investissement scolaire important des élèves du second degré, essentiellement différencié selon leur niveau scolaire*, Note d'information n°20.42, Ministère de l'Éducation nationale, de la Jeunesse et des Sports, https://www.education.gouv.fr/confinement-un-investissement-scolaire-important-des-eleves-du-second-degre-essentiellement-307441. [19]

Direction de l'évaluation, de la prospective et de la performance (DEPP) (2020), "Evaluations 2020 Repères CP, CE1 : Premiers résultats", *Série Études*, No. 2020-E04, novembre 2020, Ministère de l'Education nationale, de la Jeunesse et des Sports, Paris, https://www.education.gouv.fr/evaluations-2020-reperes-cp-ce1-premiers-resultats-307122. [29]

Direction de l'évaluation, de la prospective et de la performance (DEPP) (2020), "Évaluations de début de sixième 2020 : Premiers résultats", *Série Études*, No. 2020-E05, novembre 2020, Ministère de l'Education nationale, de la Jeunesse et des Sports, Paris, https://www.education.gouv.fr/evaluations-de-debut-de-sixieme-2020-premiers-resultats-307125. [24]

Direction de l'évaluation de la prospective et de la performance (DEPP) (2020), *Continuité pédagogique - période de mars à mai 2020 - enquêtes de la DEPP auprès des familles et des personnels de l'Éducation nationale – premiers résultats, Document de travail n°2020-E03*, Ministère de l'Education nationale, de la Jeunesse et des Sports, https://www.education.gouv.fr/continuite-pedagogique-periode-de-mars-mai-2020-enquetes-de-la-depp-aupres-des-familles-et-des-305262. [2]

Education Endowment Foundation (2021), *Best evidence on impact of Covid-19 on pupil attainment: Research examining the potential impact of school closures on the attainment gap*, https://educationendowmentfoundation.org.uk/eef-support-for-schools/covid-19-resources/best-evidence-on-impact-of-school-closures-on-the-attainment-gap/. [38]

Engzell, P., A. Frey and M. Verhagen (2020), *Learning Loss Due to School Closures During the COVID-19 Pandemic*, Center for Open Science, http://dx.doi.org/10.31235/osf.io/ve4z7. [32]

Gadermann, A., K. Thomson, C. Richardson, M. Gagné, C. McAuliffe, S. Hirani and E. Jenkins (2021), "Examining the impacts of the COVID-19 pandemic on family mental health in Canada: findings from a national cross-sectional study", *BMJ Open*, Vol. 11/1, p. e042871, http://dx.doi.org/10.1136/bmjopen-2020-042871. [9]

Gore, J., L. Fray, A. Miller, J. Harris and W. Taggart (2021), "The impact of COVID-19 on student learning in New South Wales primary schools: an empirical study", *The Australian Educational Researcher*, Vol. 48/4, pp. 605-637, http://dx.doi.org/10.1007/s13384-021-00436-w. [25]

Horowitz, J. (2020), *Lower-income parents most concerned about their children falling behind amid COVID-19 school closures, Fact Tank April 15, 2020*, Pew Research Centre, https://www.pewresearch.org/fact-tank/2020/04/15/lower-income-parents-most-concerned-about-their-children-falling-behind-amid-covid-19-school-closures/. [15]

INVALSI (2021), *I Risultati delle Prove INVALSI 2021*, https://www.invalsiopen.it/risultati/risultati-prove-invalsi-2021/. [31]

Johnson, A. and M. Kuhfeld (2020), *Fall 2019 to fall 2020 MAP Growth attrition analysis. Technical Brief*, NWEA, https://www.nwea.org/content/uploads/2020/11/Technical-brief-Fall-2019-to-fall-2020-MAP-Growth-attrition-analysis-NOV2020.pdf. [33]

Jones, J. (2020), *Social Factors Most Challenging in COVID-19 Distance Learning, Gallup Panel, 11-24 May 2020*, https://news.gallup.com/poll/312566/social-factors-challenging-covid-distance-learning.aspx. [18]

Jones, J. (2020), *Amid School Closures, Children Feeling Happiness, Boredom, Gallup Panel, 25 May-8 June 2020*, https://news.gallup.com/poll/306140/amid-school-closures-children-feeling-happiness-boredom.aspx. [4]

Kogan, V. and S. Lavertu (2021), *The COVID-19 Pandemic and Student Achievement on Ohio's Third-Grade English Language Arts Assessment*, http://glenn.osu.edu/educational-governance/reports/reports-attributes/ODE_ThirdGradeELA_KL_1-27-2021.pdf. [35]

Kuhfeld, M., E. Ruzek, A. Johnson, B. Tarasawa and K. Lewis (2020), *Technical appendix for: Learning during COVID-19: Initial findings on students' reading and math achievement and growth*, NWEA, https://www.nwea.org/content/uploads/2020/11/Technical-brief-Technical-appendix-for-Learning-during-COVID-19-Initial-findings-on-students-reading-and-math-achievement-and-growth-NOV2020.pdf. [34]

Luijten, M., M. van Muilekom, L. Teela, T. Polderman, C. Terwee, J. Zijlmans, L. Klaufus, A. Popma, K. Oostrom, H. van Oers and L. Haverman (2021), "The impact of lockdown during the COVID-19 pandemic on mental and social health of children and adolescents", *Quality of Life Research*, http://dx.doi.org/10.1007/s11136-021-02861-x. [6]

Maldonado, J. and K. De Witte (2021), "The effect of school closures on standardised student test outcomes", *British Educational Research Journal*, http://dx.doi.org/10.1002/berj.3754. [28]

Marken, S. and T. Clayton (2020), "Parents' and Students' Thoughts on Support Needed This Fall", *Gallup Blog August 27, 2020*, https://news.gallup.com/opinion/gallup/317957/parents-students-thoughts-support-needed-fall.aspx. [20]

NHS Digital (2020), *Mental Health of Children and Young People in England, 2020 - Wave 1 follow up to the 2017 survey, Main Report*, https://files.digital.nhs.uk/AF/AECD6B/mhcyp_2020_rep_v2.pdf. [8]

NHS Digital (2020), *Mental Health of Children and Young People in England, 2020: Wave 1 follow up to the 2017 survey*, https://digital.nhs.uk/data-and-information/publications/statistical/mental-health-of-children-and-young-people-in-england/2020-wave-1-follow-up/data-sets. [1]

Office for National Statistics (ONS) (2020), *Coronavirus and homeschooling in Great Britain: April to June 2020. Analysis of homeschooling in Great Britain during the coronavirus (COVID-19) pandemic from the Opinions and Lifestyle Survey*, https://www.ons.gov.uk/peoplepopulationandcommunity/educationandchildcare/articles/coronavirusandhomeschoolingingreatbritain/apriltojune2020. [11]

Ravens-Sieberer, U., A. Kaman, M. Erhart, J. Devine, R. Schlack and C. Otto (2021), "Impact of the COVID-19 pandemic on quality of life and mental health in children and adolescents in Germany", *European Child & Adolescent Psychiatry*, http://dx.doi.org/10.1007/s00787-021-01726-5. [7]

Renaissance Learning, Education Policy Institute (2021), *Understanding Progress in the 2020/21 Academic Year, Complete findings from the Autumn term: June 2021*, Department for Education, https://assets.publishing.service.gov.uk/government/uploads/system/uploads/attachment_data/file/994350/Understanding_Progress_in_the_2020_21_Academic_Year_Report_2.pdf. [27]

Rose, S., L. Twist, P. Lord, S. Rutt, K. Badr, C. Hope and B. Styles (2021), *Impact of school closures and subsequent support strategies on attainment and socio-emotional well-being in Key Stage 1: Interim Paper 1*, National Foundation for Educational Research (NFER), Slough, https://educationendowmentfoundation.org.uk/public/files/Publications/Covid-19_Resources/Impact_of_school_closures_KS1_interim_findings_paper_-_Jan_2021.pdf. [26]

Schult, J., N. Mahler, B. Fauth and M.A. Lindner (2021), *Did Students Learn Less During the COVID-19 Pandemic? Reading and Mathematics Competencies Before and After the First Pandemic Wave*, Center for Open Science, http://dx.doi.org/10.31234/osf.io/pqtgf. [23]

Thierry, X., B. Geay, A. Pailhé, N. Berthomier, J. Camus, N. Cauchi-Duval, J-L. Lanoë, S. Octobre, J. Pagis, L. Panico, T. Siméon, A. Solaz et l'équipe SAPRIS (2021), *Les enfants à l'épreuve du premier confinement*, Institut national d'études démographiques (Ined), https://www.ined.fr/fichier/s_rubrique/31037/585.enfants.confinement.population.societes.janvier.2021.fr.pdf. [3]

Tomasik, M., L. Helbling and U. Moser (2020), "Educational gains of in-person vs. distance learning in primary and secondary schools: A natural experiment during the COVID -19 pandemic school closures in Switzerland", *International Journal of Psychology*, Vol. 56/4, pp. 566-576, http://dx.doi.org/10.1002/ijop.12728. [37]

University of Southern California (USC) (2020), *Understanding Coronavirus in America Tracking Survey – Methodology and Select Crosstab Results UAS 242*, Wave 4 April 29-May 26, 2020, University of Southern California, Dornsife Center for Economic and Social Research, https://uasdata.usc.edu/index.php. [16]

Viner, R., S. Russell, R. Saulle, H. Croker, C. Stansfeld, J. Packer, D. Nicholls, A-L. Goddings, C. Bonell, L. Hudson, S. Hope, N. Schwalbe, A. Morgan, S. Minozzi (2021), *Impacts of school closures on physical and mental health of children and young people: a systematic review*, Cold Spring Harbor Laboratory, http://dx.doi.org/10.1101/2021.02.10.21251526. [36]

Wößmann, L., V. Freundl, E. Grewenig, P. Lergetporer, K. Werner and L. Zierow (2020), "Bildung in der Coronakrise: Wie haben die Schulkinder die Zeit der Schulschließungen verbracht, und welche Bildungsmaßnahmen befürworten die Deutschen?", *ifo Schnelldienst*, Vol. 73/9, pp. 25-39, https://www.ifo.de/publikationen/2020/aufsatz-zeitschrift/bildung-der-coronakrise-wie-haben-die-schulkinder-die-zeit. [13]

Notes

[1] See Viner et al. (2021[36]) for a review of studies on this topic. Most of the studies reviewed covering the incidence of mental health symptoms among children during lockdowns were based on convenience samples. Only one "high quality" study based on a representative sample is cited. However, even this study provides no information on its sampling strategy. For this reason, its findings are not reported in this report.

[2] An individual's perception and subjective evaluation of their health and well-being.

[3] Three quarters (76%) of parents were satisfied with the communication to support learning from their child(ren)'s school(s) (University of Southern California (USC), 2020[16]). High proportions of parents rated their child(ren)'s school as doing an excellent or good job in terms of teachers availability to answer questions (77%), communication about the distance education programme from the superintendent and/or principal (71%), provision of materials and equipment needed for the child to do schoolwork (75%) and communication about specific assignments from teachers (72%) as doing an excellent or good job in terms of teachers availability to answer questions (77%), communication about the distance education programme from the superintendent and/or principal (71%), provision of materials and equipment needed for the child to do schoolwork (75%) and communication about specific assignments from teachers (72%) (Jones, 2020[18]).

[4] Other studies have been published [see Tomasik, Helbling and Moser (2020[37]), Curriculum Associates (2020[39]), and the list provided in Education Endowment Foundation (2021[38])]. Many of these studies do not provide detailed information on study samples and methods and their results have not been reported included for this reason.

[5] The effects of selection biases and non-response on the representativeness of the results are argued to be negligible by the authors of all the studies concerned.

[6] See, also, the discussion in Engzell, Frey and Verhagen (2020[32]). For Kogan and Lavertu (2021[35]), average year-to-year student achievement gains in reading between second and third grade are approximately 0.6 standard deviations.

[7] Nine weeks of the normal school year including two weeks of holidays over Easter.

[8] Falls are also observed in the Dutch data set. For example, a fall between mid- and end-year performance in reading language and spelling was observed in 2017 (Engzell, Frey and Verhagen, 2020[32], Table A6).

[9] The evidence of the NFER study in England (Rose et al., 2021, p. 10[26]) is particularly unconvincing. The 2017 comparison sample "does not provide data on the performance of disadvantaged and non-disadvantaged pupils". The authors, instead, compare the standardised achievement gap observed among the 2020 sample with that derived from another assessment carried out in 2019 to estimate whether the gap has grown.

[10] See, for example, the results reported for Baden-Württemberg by Schult et al. (2021[23]). See also results for studies such as PISA (Programme for International Student Assessment), TIMMS (Trends in International Mathematics and Science Study) and PIRLS (Progress in International Reading Literacy Study).

5 Summary and conclusions

This chapter summarises the main methodology and findings of the report. Limiting its conclusions to information drawn on studies based on probability samples in the few countries that carried them out during the first wave of lockdowns, the chapter reviews the main findings concerning: schooling and delivery of educational content during the lockdowns; how the lockdown affected the parental employment situation; the impact on family's well-being and health; the impact on academic progress. It then concludes and calls for caution and patience in establishing (and also estimating) the possible impact of school closures on academic achievement.

Introduction

What we know about the experience of education during the first wave of school closures of April to June 2020 is constrained by a shortage of good quality empirical data and the fact that the "good" data that exist are partial and often not entirely comparable. This reflects the sudden and unexpected nature of the COVID-19 pandemic and the fact that the restrictions associated with lockdowns created less than ideal conditions for the conduct of survey-based research. In order to study the behaviour and attitudes of individuals during lockdowns, new data collections had to be put in place or existing collections and instruments revised. New questions had to be developed to collect information on phenomena such as remote (or home-based) schooling, teleworking, furlough and the adoption of recommended health behaviours. These needed to be developed quickly without sufficient time for testing. Probability sampling was difficult due to time constraints and the absence of appropriate sample frames. Methodological shortcuts and compromises were often adopted and data quality commonly sacrificed in the name of timeliness. The use of open access or "participative" online surveys was commonplace. In the case of surveys based on probability samples, response rates were often low. Surprisingly few national statistical offices or education ministries undertook special data collections related to the pandemic and its effects using probability samples. National testing programmes in schools scheduled during this period often did not proceed or proceeded with reduced participation by schools and students.

The information presented in this report is taken from sources that maintained minimum quality standards regarding the collection of data, particularly regarding sampling. At the same time, it reflects the limitations of the available data: the small number of countries/regions for which "good" data are available (primarily Australia, Canada, Germany, Flanders, France, Ireland, Italy, the Netherlands, the United Kingdom and the United States), the variation in the coverage and treatment of different topics in the different surveys and the limited comparability of information collected on similar topics. Obvious caution must be exercised in generalising from the experience of school students, their families and the wider population as reported in these countries, especially to low- and middle-income countries (where the duration of closures was often longer and the challenge of putting alternative delivery arrangements in place far greater). That being said, these data provide an important, if imperfect and incomplete, insight into the educational experience of schoolchildren and their families during the school closures and lockdowns of March-June 2020.

What do we know?

Schooling during the first wave of lockdowns

Duration of school closures

The duration of school closures over the period February to end-June 2020 (the end of the school year in the northern hemisphere) was between 0-19 weeks (including vacations) in OECD countries depending on the level of schooling (Figure 2.1). Net of school holidays and other public holidays in this period (around 2-3 weeks in most countries), closures meant the substitution of 4-9 weeks of face-to-face instruction with home-based learning in the majority of OECD countries.

Delivery

The use of online tools and platforms represented the predominant mode of delivery of lessons and instructional material for students undertaking their schooling at home as well as for communication between teachers and students. Hardcopy or paper-based materials continued to be used, though by a minority of students with considerable variation between countries. The reliance on online tools and resources increased with the age and year level of schoolchildren. The use of live online classes or interactions with teachers was rather limited.

Adjustments to the content of instruction

There is evidence that teachers adjusted the content and focus of instruction to reflect the new circumstances of learning. Teachers may have placed more emphasis on preserving pupils link with learning and reviewing content already covered earlier in the year than following the planned curriculum and introducing new content.

Time spent on schoolwork

The time spent at home on schoolwork by children was about half of what they would have spent in classroom-based instruction in normal times. A by no means negligible proportion of pupils (up to 20% in some countries) may have stopped their education altogether during this period and undertaken no schoolwork at all. There was considerable variation in the time spent on schoolwork between individual students.

Role of parents

During school closures, parents played an important role in supporting and supervising their children's education, particularly in the case of younger children who were less likely to be able to work unsupervised. Children in secondary education, particularly those at upper secondary level tended to work autonomously. Most, though by no means all, parents reported that they spent more time assisting children with schoolwork during school closures than in "normal" times. The average amount of time devoted by parents to support and supervise schoolwork was of relatively short duration and more time was spend on younger than older children. While many parents felt comfortable in supporting their children's education at home, a large proportion did not – at least half, if not more, in the countries in which information is available.

Difficulties faced by children regarding education

When asked about the reasons for which children experienced difficulty in continuing their education at home, the problems most commonly cited by parents and teachers were of a psychological and social nature such as lack of motivation, loneliness, etc. Difficulties related to access to the technology needed to communicate electronically with schools and teachers and access online educational resources were experienced by a significant minority of children even if most children in the countries for which data are available had access to Internet connections and the necessary devices to continue their schooling online.

The home environment

The period of confinement was a period of stress for many parents and adults more generally. In particular, the levels of anxiety experienced by adults increased considerably at the start of lockdowns and remained above pre-lockdown levels even after lockdowns had been ended. Lockdowns and home schooling created some conflicts and tensions in some households but, overall, the appreciation of the effect of lockdowns on family life was positive and relationships between parents and children were not unduly affected. In the vast majority of cases, parents reported that relationships with children remained unchanged, and the share of parents reporting that relationships with children improved outweighs the share of those for whom relationships deteriorated.

The chances of children either having contracted the COVID-19 virus themselves or living in a household in which their parents/guardians or siblings had been infected were generally low but varied considerably by country and region within countries. Among adults, infection rates varied across occupational categories.

Lockdowns resulted in considerable change to the working arrangements and employment situation of a large proportion of employed adults. The proportion of adults working from home increased significantly, with between 30-50% of employees who worked paid hours, working from home. In addition, a considerable proportion of employed adults (employees and the self-employed) were temporarily inactive due to business closures or reductions in activity. In some countries, this represented around one-third of employed adults. In others, unemployment rose dramatically. Financial stress was experienced by a minority of families, possibly reflecting the fact that considerable public support was available for both inactive workers and the unemployed in the countries for which data are available.

The changes to working arrangements had mixed consequences for families with school age children. On the one hand, job losses, and temporary lay-offs created stresses for the parents involved – reductions in income (though job retentions schemes and increases in unemployment benefits reduced their financial consequences for many) and concerns about their continued employment and professional future. On the other, presence at home due to unemployment, temporary layoff or enforced home/telework made it easier to deal with the presence of children at home and to find the time to support children's education.

For many parents, the adjustment that they needed to make to their working hours (actual hours of work and distribution over the day) to accommodate the presence of children at home was reduced hours. Parents on temporary layoff or working reduced or zero hours were available to provide childcare and assist their children's schooling and many parents working at home had more flexibility to reorganise their working hours than they might otherwise have had. Nevertheless, a significant minority of parents had to adjust their employment arrangements due to their increased responsibilities for the care and supervision of infants and school age children during school closures (e.g. reduced or changed working hours, stopped work altogether or took leave). Overall, however, most parents were able to manage to balance the competing demands of work and the care of and support for their children.

Outcomes: Psychological well-being and academic progress

Psychological well-being

Lockdowns and school closures involved their lot of inconvenience, difficulties and stress for school age children, but little more. The psychological well-being of most children did not decline to any great extent during lockdown compared to the situation prior to lockdown. The proportion of school-age children experiencing serious or severe symptoms of mental or psychological disorders may have risen during the period of lockdown. However, the proportion concerned was relatively small. Most school-age children, both before and during the period of lockdowns, did not display such symptoms.

Perceptions of the impact of school closures on children's education

Parents offer a rather mixed evaluation of the impact of lockdowns and school closures on children's development and educational progress. High levels of appreciation of the work of schools and teachers during school closures was accompanied by concerns regarding the effects of lockdowns and school closures on children's educational and social development. While a link with school was maintained by most children and there were some positive features of home schooling for children such as increasing autonomy in learning and the discovery of new methods of learning, many parents were concerned about lack of progress in some subjects and the possibility that their children were falling behind.

Academic progress

There is limited and conflicting evidence from standardised tests regarding students' learning progress during school closures compared to progress in "normal" conditions. The quality of the data varies somewhat, with a number of studies based on data from non-representative samples of schools or data that are affected by high rates of non-participation by schools and students. The differences observed between the performance of students tested in 2020 or in early 2021 with students in the same year of school in previous years range from small increases to large falls (the scale of which are, in some cases, implausibly large) depending on the countries, the year groups and the subjects concerned.[1] At the very least, the available results in countries where relevant studies are available suggest that it should not be assumed that the school closures of March-June 2020 had a large negative impact on student progress and achievement.

The impact of social background

Understandable concerns have been raised regarding the differential impact of school closures on schoolchildren from different social backgrounds and the possibility that differences in the home situation of children from disadvantaged social backgrounds would exacerbate existing inequalities in achievement. There is little doubt that the negative impact of the pandemic has been greater among disadvantaged populations.

Rates of infection and COVID-19-related deaths varied across different social and occupational groups. In particular, infection and death rates were higher among the population living in areas of low as opposed to high socio-economic status (SES) in England and France and among certain ethnic groups, for example Blacks and Asians in the United Kingdom, first and second generation non-European immigrants in France and Blacks and Hispanics/Latinos in the United States. At the same time, infection rates were positively related to education and higher among people at the top and bottom of the income distribution than in the middle. In particular, this reflects the higher infection rates among frontline health workers than among other workers. Frontline health workers represent a highly heterogeneous group that includes both highly educated and highly paid workers (e.g. doctors and other medical professionals) and low educated and poorly paid workers (nursing assistants and cleaners in hospitals).

The effects of lockdowns on the employment situation of workers also differed by occupation. The incidence of temporary lay-offs was higher in lower status than higher status occupations (e.g. among manual workers as opposed to professionals) with the reverse being true regarding the incidence of home/telework. Loss of income associated with lockdowns was concentrated among low income groups as a result. The incidence of mental health problems such as anxiety was also higher among adults in lower status occupations and among those with lower incomes and who had seen their financial situation worsen due to lockdowns.

In terms of children's education, children from less advantaged socio-economic backgrounds had greater difficulties than other children with access to the devices and connectivity necessary to continue their education at home. Students who completely dropped out of education during the period of lockdown appear more likely to come disproportionately from disadvantaged backgrounds and to have had a prior history of difficulties with schooling.

In the countries covered, there is limited evidence of family SES having an impact on the amount of time spent on schoolwork or the amount of time parents spent assisting children: children from all backgrounds seem to have devoted more or less the same time to their schoolwork and to have received the same amount of parental assistance. In fact, students from higher SES families sometimes received less support than those from lower status families. This may reflect the fact that parents in higher status jobs had less time to support their children as they were more likely to have been working (rather than being on temporary layoff or unemployed) during lockdowns than adults with less education in lower status occupations. It may be possible that the effectiveness of the assistance offered was dependent of the level of education of parents. Importantly, however, the interest in and willingness to provide support was equally distributed across households from all backgrounds.

The evidence regarding the evolution of achievement gaps between children from different social backgrounds among students experiencing lockdowns and school closures in 2020 compared to their peers in previous years is mixed. Both little change in the size of achievement gaps related to social background and significant growth has been found.

In summary

The picture offered of the experience and consequences in high-income countries of the first wave of school closures of March-June 2020 in this report is a relatively optimistic one. The lockdowns and associated closures of schools implemented in response to the arrival of the COVID-19 pandemic represented a sudden and unprecedented event for which school authorities, teachers, parents and students were unprepared. Nevertheless, distance and remote education arrangements were put in place at short notice in emergency conditions.[2] This allowed education to continue at home for the majority of children and a form of in-person instruction to be offered to children with special needs and the children of parents with no other care options such as the children of "essential" workers. While few would disagree that the distance/remote education arrangements put in place represented a less than perfect substitute for normal classes, they ensured that most, though not all, children continued to have a connection with teachers and their schools. For the most part, teachers, students and parents adapted to the new arrangements. Most teachers continued to teach and most students continued to learn. Most parents were able to assist their children with their education if needed. Such a dramatic and sudden disruption to schooling arrangements could hardly be expected to have been without some impact on students' learning, especially when accompanied by a health crisis and the disruptive effect of lockdowns on every aspect of social and economic life. At this point, however, the evidence regarding the impact on academic progress is inconclusive and far from universally negative. Even if definitive conclusions cannot be drawn at this point, the negative consequences for the academic or broader development and mental health of schoolchildren may have been modest in scale and impact. Moreover, the report also highlights that there may also be positive lessons to be drawn from the health crisis as far as schooling is concerned. At least, the possible positive experiences from the lockdowns and its alternative mode of schooling should be considered when experimenting and reforming school provision during and after the pandemic.

Looking ahead

Assuming some effects on student's learning, an important question is whether students affected will be able to "catch up" on or consolidate any gaps in their learning resulting from the disruption to their schooling during the period of school closures. The scale of any on-going impact of the disruption to students' education caused by school closures on their academic performance and progress will be related to, among other things: (1) the relevance of what they "missed" for their subsequent educational progress, (2) the opportunities they have and support they are given to catch up on any learning "gaps" resulting from reduced instruction and learning during school closures, and (3) the evolution of the COVID-19 pandemic and the measures implemented to manage it, including further school closures and the quality of the remote education received during these periods.

Regarding missed instruction, for many students failing to cover some elements of the curriculum in some subjects may not matter for their subsequent progress (or, *a fortiori*, for their "human capital" when they enter the labour market). By no means all the content covered in a subject in one year is a necessary pre-requisite for subsequent progress in either the subject area directly concerned or related areas. This is especially true at transition points (e.g. entering upper secondary school or moving from school to post-secondary studies), where students start to specialise in certain subject areas rather than others (and, therefore, "drop" some subjects). Much of what is learned in school is not "used" in later life (as is evidenced by the speed at which it is forgotten). An important component of school learning is less about the retention of particular content than "learning to learn" and being aware that one can learn.

In terms of the opportunities for catch up, consolidation of the gaps in students' education due to the disruption flowing from school closures was high on the agendas of most governments and school authorities at the start of the 2020-21 school year. OECD (2021[1], Table 3.3) reports that around three-quarters of the countries for which data were available implemented "remedial measures to reduce learning gaps" when schools reopened after the first period of closures. In France for example, the priorities for the new school year included support for students to consolidate the aspects of their programmes that they did not cover due to confinement.[3] In the United Kingdom, the Government introduced a Coronavirus (COVID-19) catch up premium and a national tutoring programme to support students and young people affected by the disruption of their education.[4] The advice offered to schools at the start of the 2020-21 school year in England was to aim "to return to the school's normal curriculum in all subjects by summer term 2021".[5] Even in the absence of specific programmes, it is likely that teachers would adjust their instruction to compensate for any content missed by students and that many parents[6] would make efforts to ensure that their children catch up, as would the students themselves (especially those in high school). This is likely to be true regardless of their socio-economic status (although their effectiveness in reaching their goals may vary).

> ### Box 5.1. Comparing the second to the first wave of school closures: Germany
>
> (Wößmann et al., 2021[2]) surveyed a representative sample of 2 000 parents in February-March 2021 to capture the experience of the second wave of school closures in Germany at the beginning of 2021. The results have been compared with their study of the first wave of school closures (Wößmann et al., 2020[3]). The findings show the extent of adaptation to closures. Compared to the first wave, students spent more time on their schoolwork than during the second school closures (4.3 hours per day against 3.6 in 2020) and less time on other activities such as reading and exercise, and screen time (down from 5.2 hours per day in 2020 to 4.6 in 2021) (Wößmann et al., 2020[3], Figure 1). Collective virtual classes were far more common (at least once a week for 74% of students in 2021 against 43% in 2020). Parents offered broadly similar ratings of the utility of school activities in 2020 and 2021 The share of parents feeling their children have learnt less than normal decreased slightly (from 64% in 2020 to 59% in 2021). Seventy-five percent of parents did not see any decline in the socio-emotional state of their children compared to before the pandemic. Some aspects of the experience changed, however, particularly regarding the family climate. The second lockdown was more stressful for both parents and their children and parents felt that it led to more family tensions than during the first school closures, even though 71% of parents still considered that the family coped well with the situation (against 86% in 2020). The overall picture offered by parents of the second wave is not very different from that of the first, notably when compared to "normal" times. It suggests that students may have made more academic progress during the second wave (as imperfect as conditions may have remained), but that both students and parents may have become more fed up with the situation.

The pandemic has continued to disrupt social and economic life into 2021. In most countries, the 2020-21 school year was disrupted, to a greater or lesser extent, by the COVID-19 pandemic and the measures put in place to control it (including further lockdowns and school closures in a number of countries). For example, in the United States, in some jurisdictions, schools remained closed during the whole school year, and the impact of those closures may have been different (both negatively and positively) to that observed during the first wave. (The evidence to assess them is however still largely missing as of September 2021.) Even in countries where schools remained open during further lockdowns (such as France), children's education was affected by the implementation of strict sanitary protocols, the closure of classes and individual schools due to cases of COVID-19 among students and staff and the introduction of "hybrid" forms of schooling alternating face-to-face and online delivery of lessons. The continuing disruption is likely to have complicated the task of consolidating any learning gaps arising from the March-June 2020 school closures and, possibly, to have created additional learning gaps.

At the same time, one would expect that schools systems, teachers, parents and students learnt much from the experience of the first period of lockdown and school closures [see e.g. New South Wales (NSW) Department of Education (2020[4])] for a reflection on the experience of closures in the first half of 2020]. This may have permitted them to effectively adapt to the circumstances of life and schooling during the 2020-21 school year and limit the negative effects on teaching and learning. There is some evidence that this occurred [see Del Bono et al. (2021[5]) for the United Kingdom]. There is also evidence that teachers, parents and students changed their behaviour in subsequent lockdowns [see (Wößmann et al., 2021[2]) and Box 5.1 for an overview].

As for the psychological well-being of school age children, the question is much the same as for school achievement. Were the declines in well-being observed during the lockdowns of March-June 2020 an immediate and short-lived reaction to an extraordinary and stressful situation which were reversed as life returned to something approaching normal or were they more enduring? Again, more time and more data will be needed before this question can be answered.

This leads to the issue of data and the long-term monitoring of the consequences of the pandemic (not only for the period of school closures in the first half of 2020) on children's schooling and well-being. Surprisingly few high quality data collections were put in place during the period of school closures. This has restricted the capacity of researchers and analysts to have a good understanding what occurred during this period and of the behaviour and views of those involved and affected by closures and the disruption to school education. The collection of good data on the instructional practices and arrangements, the experience of pupils, teachers and parents and the outcomes of pupils continues to be important for the understanding of this extraordinary period and its consequences for schoolchildren's academic progress and well-being and the practice of education. It is also vital that school systems and Ministries of Education make publicly available as much of the administrative and other data regarding this period they can in easily accessible formats as well as facilitate access to relevant documentation about policies and administrative decisions during this period. Access to data from standardised tests is particularly important, not only from those that took place in 2020 and earlier years but, equally importantly, those that will take place over coming years.

In countries where national assessments did not take place or do not exist, international assessments such as those of the OECD Programme of International Student Assessment (PISA) combined with national data on the conditions of schooling during the pandemic will allow one to better assess the impact of the crisis. International assessments will also give us a better idea of the impact of the pandemic and of responses to it across countries, and notably whether it led to an increase in the achievement gaps between countries, notably high and middle-low income countries.

References

Del Bono, E., L. Fumagalli, A. Holford and B. Rabe (2021), *Coping with school closures: Changes in home-schooling during COVID-19*, Institute for Social and Economic Research (ISER) Report July 2021, University of Essex, https://www.iser.essex.ac.uk/files/news/2021/little-inequality-homeschool/coping-with-school-closures.pdf. [5]

Hanushek, E. and L. Woessmann (2020), "The economic impacts of learning losses", *OECD Education Working Papers*, No. 225, OECD Publishing, Paris, https://dx.doi.org/10.1787/21908d74-en. [6]

NSW Department of Education (2020), *Lessons from the COVID-19 Pandemic January–July 2020*, https://www.education.nsw.gov.au/content/dam/main-education/en/home/covid-19/lessons-from-the-covid-19-pandemic-jan-july-2020.pdf. [4]

OECD (2021), *The State of School Education: One Year into the COVID Pandemic*, OECD Publishing, Paris, https://dx.doi.org/10.1787/201dde84-en. [1]

Wößmann, L., V. Freundl, E. Grewenig, P. Lergetporer, K. Werner and L. Zierow (2021), "Bildung erneut im Lockdown: Wie verbrachten Schulkinder die Schulschließungen Anfang 2021?", *ifo Schnelldienst*, Vol. 74/5, pp. 36-52, https://www.ifo.de/DocDL/sd-2021-05-woessmann-etal-corona-schulschliessungen.pdf. [2]

Wößmann, L., V. Freundl, E. Grewenig, P. Lergetporer, K. Werner and L. Zierow (2020), "Bildung in der Coronakrise: Wie haben die Schulkinder die Zeit der Schulschließungen verbracht, und welche Bildungsmaßnahmen befürworten die Deutschen?", *ifo Schnelldienst*, Vol. 73/09, pp. 25-39, https://www.ifo.de/publikationen/2020/aufsatz-zeitschrift/bildung-de. [3]

Notes

[1] A plea regarding terminology. Much of the discussion regarding the possible effects of school closures on students' academic progress has been framed in terms of *"learning loss"*. This misrepresentation of a situation that is better understood as one of (possibly) reduced learning gains relative to those expected in normal circumstances. The fact students did not attend school in person and that remote instruction was substituted for face-to-face instruction for a period did not mean that that they did not learn anything or, worse, that they somehow unlearnt what they had learnt up to that point. However, to the extent that learning inputs were reduced compared to normal times during this period or the effectiveness and efficiency of learning was reduced, students may have learnt less than they would otherwise have done.

[2] See the 53 "education continuity stories" from 34 countries posted by the OECD and the World Bank on their website that document different types of innovations or contingency plans to adapt to the school closures: https://oecdedutoday.com/coronavirus/continuity-stories/. They were documented in real time as part of a joing initiative by the OECD, the World Bank, Harvard Global Education Innovation Initative and HundrED. They will jointly be published by the OECD and the World Bank.

[3] As an example: « Au lycée, la rentrée 2020 se place sous le signe de l'identification des besoins propres à chaque élève et des réponses personnalisées qui peuvent y être apportées, avec pour objectif de résorber les écarts qui ont pu naître pendant la crise sanitaire ». "In upper secondary schools, the start of the 2020 school year has as its focus the identification of the individual needs of each student and the personalised support that can be offered to overcome the gaps in learning that may have developed during the health crisis." https://eduscol.education.fr/cid152895/rentree-2020-priorites-et-positionnement.html

[4] https://www.gov.uk/guidance/coronavirus-COVID-19-catch-up-premium

[5] It was acknowledged that: "Substantial modification to the curriculum may be needed at the start of the year, so teaching time should be prioritised to address significant gaps in pupils' knowledge with the aim of returning to the school's normal curriculum content by no later than summer term 2021."

[6] Acknowledging that the efforts of parents may well vary according to their socio-economic status.

Annex A. Main survey data sources

| 101

Table A A.1. Main survey data sources

Country	Study name	Sponsor	Target population(s)	Content	Data collection dates	Documentation on methods
Australia	Household Impacts of COVID-19 Survey	Australian Bureau of Statistics	Adults aged 18 years and older resident in private dwellings	Omnibus	Bi-monthly from April-June 2020 then monthly	
Canada	Assessing the Impacts of COVID-19 on Mental Health	University of British Columbia, the Canadian Mental Health Association (Canada) the Mental Health Foundation (UK)	Adults aged 18 years and over	Mental health	14-29 May 2020	https://www.sciencedirect.com/science/article/pii/S0091743520303649
France	Continuité pédagogique - période de mars à mai 2020 - enquêtes de la DEPP auprès des familles et des personnels de l'Éducation nationale	Ministère de l'Éducation nationale, de la Jeunesse et des Sports, Direction de l'évaluation, de la prospective et de la performance (DEPP)	a) Secondary students in public and private schools and their parents b) Primary and secondary school teachers in public and private schools c) School principals	Education	May-June 2020	https://www.education.gouv.fr/continuite-pedagogique-periode-de-mars-mai-2020-enquetes-de-la-depp-aupres-des-familles-et-des-305262
	CoviPrev	Santé Publique France	Persons aged 18 years and over	Mental health and health behaviours	22 waves of data collection from 23-25 March 2020	https://www.santepubliquefrance.fr/etudes-et-enquetes/COVID-19-une-enquete-pour-suivre-l-evolution-des-comportements-et-de-la-sante-mentale-pendant-l-epidemie
	COronavirus et CONfinement : Enquête Longitudinale (Coconel)	UMR Vitrome, Centre d'investigation clinique Cochin-Pasteur, l'École des hautes études en santé publique (EHESP), l'Observatoire régional de la santé Sud-Provence-Alpes-Côte d'Azur	Persons aged 18 years and over	Attitudes, beliefs, behaviours, relationships during confinement	9 waves of data collection – 27-29 March to 19-23 June 2020	http://www.orspaca.org/COVID19/projets-recherche/coconel
	EpiCov	Inserm, Direction de la recherche, des études, de l'évaluation et des statistiques (DREES), Ministère des Solidarités et de la Santé	Adults aged 15 years and over	Immunity to COVID-19; home and life situation during confinement	2 May-2 June 2020 (first wave) November 2020 (second wave)	https://drees.solidarites-sante.gouv.fr/communique-de-presse/communique-de-presse/epicov-connaitre-le-statut-immunitaire-de-la-population

Country	Study name	Sponsor	Target population(s)	Content	Data collection dates	Documentation on methods
Germany	COPSY (Impact of COVID-19 on psychological health) study	University of Hamburg and the Ministry of Health and Consumer Protection Hamburg	Families with children and adolescents aged 7-17 years	Mental health	26 May to 10 June 2020	https://doi.org/10.1007/s00787-021-01726-5
	ifo Education Barometer 2020 and 20211	Ifo Institute, financed by Deutsche Forschunggemeinschaft (DFG)	Adults aged 18-69 years	Education	3 June-1 July 2020 (2020) and 27 May-22 June 2021 (2021)	https://www.ifo.de/publikationen/2020/aufsatz-zeitschrift/bildung-der-coronakrise-wie-haben-die-schulkinder-die-zeit
	Sozio-oekonomischen Panels (SOEP) and Sonderbefragung des Sozio-oekonomischen Panels (SOEP-CoV)	DIW Berlin	Parents with children aged 7 to 18 years (Education); Persons aged 17 and over (Health)	Education; Health	1 April-4 July 2020 (Education); 1-26 April 2020 (Health)	https://www.diw.de/documents/publikationen/73/diw_01.c.804515.de/20-47-1.pdf https://www.diw.de/documents/publikationen/73/diw_01.c.791307.de/diw_sp1087.pdf
	Studie eGovernment MONITOR 2020	Initiative D21 and Technischen Universität München (TUM), carried out by Kantar	Adults aged 18 and over using the Internet in private dwellings	Digitalisation; Education	1-30 June 2020	https://www.kantar.com/de/inspiration/d21/erfolgreiches-homeschooling-waehrend-corona
Ireland	Social Impact of COVID-19 Survey, August 2020: The Reopening of Schools	Central Statistical Office	Adults aged 15 years and over resident in private dwellings	Education	13-19 August 2020	https://www.cso.ie/en/releasesandpublications/ep/p-sic19ros/socialimpactofCOVID-19surveyaugust2020thereopeningofschools/backgroundnotes/
	Employment and Life Effects of COVID-19 April 2020 (Supplement to LFS)	Central Statistical Office	Adults aged 15 years and over resident in private dwellings	Employment, and other life effects	8-23 April 2020	https://www.cso.ie/en/releasesandpublications/er/elec19/employmentandlifeeffectsofCOVID-19/
Netherlands (The)	n/a	Amsterdam UMC	Children and adolescents 8-18 years of age	Mental health	10 April and 5 May 2020	https://doi.org/10.1007/s11136-021-02861-x
Switzerland	Swiss Household Panel – COVID-19 Study	Swiss Centre of Expertise in the Social Sciences FORS	Persons aged 14-99 years	Omnibus	12 May – 26 June 2020	https://forscenter.ch/working-papers/first-results-of-the-swiss-household-panel-COVID-19-study/

Country	Study name	Sponsor	Target population(s)	Content	Data collection dates	Documentation on methods
United Kingdom	Opinions and Lifestyle Survey (COVID-19 module)	National Office of Statistics	Adults aged 16 years and over resident in private dwellings	Omnibus	Weekly from 20 March 2020	Opinions and Lifestyle Survey QMI - Office for National Statistics
	Understanding Society COVID-19 Survey	Institute for Social and Economic Research, University of Essex	All members aged 16 years and older, as of April 2020, of the main Understanding Society samples[1]	Omnibus	6 waves: April, May, June, July, September and November 2020	https://www.understandingsociety.ac.uk/documentation/COVID-19
	NHS Digital		Participants (children and their parents) in the Mental Health of Children and Young People (MHCYP) 2017 survey who consented to recontact for further research. Age range 5-22 years	Health, social functioning, impact of COVID-19 on family life	3 July – 20 August 2020	https://files.digital.nhs.uk/D1/D411D3/mhcyp_2020_meth.pdf
United States	Supplemental data measuring the effects of the coronavirus (COVID-19) pandemic on the labor market	Bureau of Labor Statistics	Adults aged 16 years and over	Labour market	Monthly from May 2020	https://www.bls.gov/cps/effects-of-the-coronavirus-COVID-19-pandemic.htm#table1
	Household Pulse Survey	US Census Bureau	Adults aged 15 years and over resident in private dwellings	Labour market, education, health	Phase 1 – weekly from 23 April to 21 July 2020	https://www.census.gov/programs-surveys/household-pulse-survey/technical-documentation.html
	Gallup Panel	Gallup	Parents of children under the age of 18 and who are members of the Gallup Panel[2].	Education	March-June 2020	https://news.gallup.com/poll/306140/amid-school-closures-children-feeling-happiness-boredom.aspx
	Gallup Panel	NewSchools Venture fund/Gallup	a) Parents of children under the age of 18 and who are members of the Gallup Panel[2]. b) Children in grades 3-12 of consenting panel members	Education	22 July-5 August 2020	https://news.gallup.com/opinion/gallup/317957/parents-students-thoughts-support-needed-fall.aspx
	American Trends Panel	Pew Research Centre	Adults - members of the American Trends Panel[2]	Education	7-12 April 2020	https://www.pewresearch.org/internet/2020/04/30/COVID-internet-methodology/
	American Educator Panel	RAND Education and Labor	K–12 public school teachers and principals[3]	Education	27 April-11 May 2020	https://www.rand.org/pubs/research_reports/RRA168-1.html

Country	Study name	Sponsor	Target population(s)	Content	Data collection dates	Documentation on methods
United States	Understanding Coronavirus in America Tracking Survey	USC Dornsife Center for Economic and Social Research	Adults aged 18 years or more – members of the Understanding America Study panel	Omnibus	First wave 10-31 March 2020, every two weeks from 1 April 2020	https://uasdata.usc.edu/index.php

1. The Understanding Society survey or the UK Household Longitudinal Study (UKHLS) is a longitudinal study based on a representative sample of households in the United Kingdom. Respondents include all members of the sampled households aged 10 years or older.
2. Both the Gallup Panel and the American Trends Panel are nationally representative panels of randomly selected US adults.
3. The American Educator Panel is a nationally representative panel of public school teachers and school principals in the United States.

Annex B. Lockdown measures in selected countries: February-June 2020

Table A B.1. Lockdown measures: February-June 2020 – Selected countries

Country	Domain concerned	Dates	Description
Australia	Schools	24/3-early May	Schools closed. Partial resumption of in-person schooling from early May (depending on State/Territory)
	Employment	22/3-15/5	non-essential services closed (or work from home) for some sectors or categories of workers
		26/5- 30/6	non-essential businesses and services open, working from home recommended
	Stay at home	21/3-1/4	recommend not leaving house
		2/4-14/5	required not to leave house with exceptions for daily exercise, grocery shopping, and "essential" trips
		29/5-30/6	No restrictions
Canada	Schools	23/3-30/6	All schools closed
	Employment	14/3-30/6	Working from home recommended
	Stay at home	18/3-21/6	3 required not to leave house with minimal exceptions for daily exercise, grocery shopping, and "essential" trips
		22/6-30/6	2 required not to leave house with exceptions for daily exercise, grocery shopping, and "essential" trips
Flanders	Schools	16/3-11/5	All schools closed
	Employment	14/3-17/3	require closing (or work from home) for some sectors or categories of workers
		18/3-10/5	Non-essential workplaces closed (or work from home) all-but-essential workplaces (e.g. grocery stores, doctors)
		11/5-30/6	require closing (or work from home) for some sectors or categories of workers
	Stay at home	18/3-7/6	require not leaving house with exceptions for daily exercise, grocery shopping, and "essential" trips
		8/6-30/6	No restrictions
France	Schools	16/3-11/5	Primary schools closed
		16/3-19/5	Lower secondary schools closed
		16/3-25/5	Upper secondary schools closed
	Employment	17/3-10/5	Non-essential workplaces (e.g. grocery stores, doctors) closed (or work from home)
		11/5-21/6	non-essential services require closing (or work from home) for some sectors or categories of workers
		22/6-30/6	non-essential businesses and services reopen recommended working from home
	Stay at home	17/3-10/5	require not leaving house with exceptions for daily exercise, grocery shopping, and "essential" trips
		11/5-21/6	recommend not leaving house
		22/6-30/6	No restrictions
Germany	Schools	16/3-04/05	All schools closed
	Employment	22//3-30/6	non-essential services require closing (or work from home) for some sectors or categories of workers
	Stay at home	9/3-20/3	recommend not leaving house
		21/3-5/5	require not leaving house with exceptions for daily exercise, grocery shopping, and "essential" trips
		6/5-30/6	No restrictions

Country	Domain concerned	Dates	Description
Ireland	Schools	13/3-29/6	Primary schools closed
		13/3-31/5	Secondary schools closed
	Employment	12/3-26/3	Working from home recommended
		27/3-17/5	require closing (or work from home) all-but-essential workplaces (e.g. grocery stores, doctors)
		18/5-25/6	non-essential services require closing (or work from home) for some sectors or categories of workers
		26/6-30/6	Working from home recommended
	Stay at home	26/3-27/3	recommend not leaving house
		28/3-17/5	require not leaving house with exceptions for daily exercise, grocery shopping, and "essential" trips
		18/5-25/6	Recommended not leaving house
		36/6-30/6	No restrictions
The Netherlands	Schools	16/3-11/5	Primary schools closed
		16/3-2/6	Secondary schools closed
	Employment	12/3-14/3	Working from home recommended
		15/3-10/5	require closing (or work from home) all-but-essential workplaces (e.g. grocery stores, doctors)
		11/5-30/6	require closing (or work from home) for some sectors or categories of workers
	Stay at home	6/3-22/3	Recommended not to leave house
		23/3-10/5	Requirement not to leave house with exceptions for daily exercise, grocery shopping, and "essential" trips
		11/5-30/6	recommend not leaving house
Switzerland	Schools	11/3-6/5	Primary and lower secondary schools closed
		11/3-8/6	Upper secondary schools closed
	Employment	17/3-26/4	require closing (or work from home) all-but-essential workplaces (e.g. grocery stores, doctors)
		27/4-5/6	non-essential services require closing (or work from home) for some sectors or categories of workers
		6/6-30/6	Working from home recommended
	Stay at home	17/3-22/6	recommend not leaving house
		23/6-30/6	No restrictions
United Kingdom	Schools	23/3-1/6	Primary schools closed
		23/3-15/6	Secondary schools closed
	Employment	12/3-26/3	Working from home recommended
		27/3-17/5	require closing (or work from home) all-but-essential workplaces (e.g. grocery stores, doctors)
		18/5-25/6	non-essential services require closing (or work from home) for some sectors or categories of workers
		26/6-30/6	Working from home recommended
	Stay at home	13/3-21/3	recommend not leaving house
		22/3-12/5	require not leaving house with exceptions for daily exercise, grocery shopping, and "essential" trips
		13/5-30/6	recommend not leaving house
United States	Schools	24/3-	All public schools closed until end of 2020 school year
	Employment	19/3-14/6	require closing (or work from home) all-but-essential workplaces (e.g. grocery stores, doctors)
		15/6-30/6	non-essential services require closing (or work from home) for some sectors or categories of workers
	Stay at home	15/3-30/6	require not leaving house with exceptions for daily exercise, grocery shopping, and "essential" trips

Sources: (Hale et al., 2021[1]; OECD, 2021[2]); (Bacher-Hicks, Goodman and Mulhern, 2021[3], Table A3).

References

Bacher-Hicks, A., J. Goodman and C. Mulhern (2021), "Inequality in household adaptation to schooling shocks: Covid-induced online learning engagement in real time", *Journal of Public Economics*, Vol. 193, p. 104345, http://dx.doi.org/10.1016/j.jpubeco.2020.104345. [3]

Hale, T., N. Angrist, R. Goldszmidt, B. Kira, A. Petherick, T. Phillips, S. Webster, E. Cameron-Blake, L. Hallas, S. Majumdar and H. Tatlow (2021), "A global panel database of pandemic policies (Oxford COVID-19 Government Response Tracker)", *Nature Human Behaviour*, Vol. 5/4, pp. 529-538, http://dx.doi.org/10.1038/s41562-021-01079-8. [1]

OECD (2021), *The State of School Education: One Year into the COVID Pandemic*, https://doi.org/10.1787/201dde84-en. [2]

Printed in November 2021
by Rotomail Italia S.p.A., Vignate (MI) - Italy